Raising Puppies & Kids Together

Together

A Guide for Parents

Pia Silvani, CPDT and Lynn Eckhardt

t.f.h.

Raising Puppies & Kids Together

Project Team
Editor: Heather Russell-Revesz
Copy Editor: Carl Schutt
Design: Candida Tomassini

T.F.H. Publications
President/CEO: Glen S. Axelrod
Executive Vice President: Mark E. Johnson
Publisher: Christopher T. Reggio
Production Manager: Kathy Bontz

T.F.H. Publications, Inc.
One TFH Plaza
Third and Union Avenues
Neptune City, NJ 07753

Cover image ©Stockbyte

06 07 08 09 10 3 5 7 9 8 6 4 2
Printed and bound in China

Library of Congress Cataloging-in-Publication Data
Silvani, Pia.
Raising puppies and kids together : a guide for parents / Pia Silvani and Lynn Eckhardt.
p. cm.
Includes bibliographical references and index.
ISBN 0-7938-0568-6 (alk. paper)
1.   Puppies. 2. Dogs-Social aspects. 3. Children and animals. I. Eckhardt, Lynn. II. Title.
SF427.S594 2005
636.7'07--dc22
2005012984

This book has been published with the intent to provide accurate and authoritative information in regard to the subject matter within. While every precaution has been taken in preparation of this book, the author and publisher expressly disclaim responsibility for any errors, omissions, or adverse effects arising from the use or application of the information contained herein. The techniques and suggestions are used at the reader's discretion and are not to be considered a substitute for veterinary care. If you suspect a medical problem consult your veterinarian.

The Leader In Responsible Animal Care For Over 50 Years!™

www.tfhpublications.com

Table of Contents

Dedication

This book is dedicated to our husbands for supporting us and temporarily giving up the precious personal time that we have with them. It is also dedicated to all of our long-past, yet ever so memorable four-legged family members who taught us so much and will always be in our hearts: Koyla, Chester, Ashley, Samantha, Jay, Akeem, and Skye. And of course our present canine companions who make waking up every day so worthwhile: Jordan, Kobe, Strider, Lance, and Guinnie. Last but not least, Pia's nephews, Bobby and Ryan, who have helped her learn how much love children can bring to you and dogs; and Lynn's children, Matthew and Sydney for providing Lynn with many great photo opportunities and all their patience while mommy spent hours at the computer.

Acknowledgments

The writing of a book is a process where so many people are involved in so many ways. We would like to start by thanking our publisher and editors for having the enthusiasm and confidence in us, and encouraging us to write this book. We both had concerns about whether or not our schedules would permit this; but when you feel passionate about a topic, you get it done!

A special thank you to all of our friends and family members who took the time to devote many hours reviewing the manuscript. Your feedback, support and encouragement are enormously appreciated.

We would like to express our sincerest appreciation to our parents who have always supported our efforts throughout our lives and told us that we could do anything we set our minds out to do.

An extra special thanks to our husbands. We both left corporate careers to do something in life that we loved—work with people and their dogs. Without the support and understanding of our husbands, we would not be where we are today.

Pia's Special Thanks

My academic mentors have not only become close friends of mine, but they will always be an inspiration to me. I am indebted to you all for your support, friendship, and what you have taught me: R.K. Anderson, Peter Borchelt, Ian Dunbar, Dan Estep, Alice Moon-Fanelli, Suzanne Hetts, Patricia McConnell, Mary Lee Nitschke, Pamela Reid, and Terry Ryan.

My colleagues and friends around the country have meant so much to me in my career. Their expertise and continued support and communication on an intellectual, as well as friendship level has been invaluable. I can't imagine not having them as part of my life. Lynn Becker, Vinny Catalano, Kathleen Chin, Dana Crevling, Jean Donaldson, Donna Duford, Sue Sternberg, Trish King, Rosemarie Vaccaro, Nancy Williams.

A big thank you to all the wonderful staff at St. Hubert's Animal Welfare Center for always supporting my efforts.

A very special thanks to Ed Sayres for believing in me and supporting my goals to help promote humane training on a greater level than could ever be expected, as well as Elizabeth McCorkle, President of St. Hubert's Animal Welfare Center, who continually fosters, supports, and encourages me to be creative in developing new programs, locally and internationally, to enable me to provide continuing education and help foster the bond between people and their dogs.

Last but not least, a special thank you to Lynn, my colleague, my friend, my co-author. You are a wonderful mother and special person. Not many people would sit at their computer night after night at 2:00 a.m. (her "free time") to write a book. Especially after spending the day with two toddlers, three dogs and a husband asking "are you done yet?"

Lynn's Special Thanks

My early involvement with dogs was training for obedience, agility, and herding competitions; as well as competing in the show ring. I would like to thank all of my teachers, past and present who have shared their knowledge and helped to make me a better handler and trainer; and gave me an understanding of dogs that you just cannot have until you really try to 'work' with them. Thank you to all of my friends for getting me interested and involved in the wonderful and exciting sport of dogs. It has been a great 20+ years and I look forward to many more!

My very special thanks goes out to all the children in my life. My own children as well as my nieces and nephews. It is truly a joy to watch children playing with and loving their dog or puppy. They have all helped me to learn a great deal more about dogs and dog behavior than I would ever have known.

How do I thank Pia? My friend and co-author. The past five years of our friendship and work together will be cherished forever. I thank her so much for her support in me and trust of my knowledge and abilities with dogs. It is not an easy task to try to take on a project such as this with another person, especially a friend. Our friendship withstood the test, as I knew it would, and I greatly look forward to future projects together!

Foreword

Well at last … The complete guide for all of those motivated moms and dads who want to be successful at the magical combination of children and puppies. There is no need for parents to wonder anymore if they can be successful in this integration of a well-adjusted child and puppy, and success will yield poignant, quality-of-life moments for every member of the family.

If you have questions, you'll find the most balanced and comprehensive answers available, and if you are at step one of the feasibility phase, the information is all here.

Pia and Lynn, with thousands of people and dogs in their client experience, make this book sparkle with easy-to-understand explanations and offer the perfect real-life example to amplify the lesson.

Of course, it is no surprise that Pia and Lynn would create the perfect book on this topic as they have thousands of fans/clients all around the country grateful for their problem-solving insight and the fun they administer with every lesson. It was just a matter of getting them to stop the demands on their time to enable their practical wisdom to be channeled into this dynamic publication.

Success for child and puppy will be a lifelong lesson in empathy, nurturing, learning, and just plain laugh-out-loud fun for everyone. And now there is no reason to wonder about the best way to approach any of the challenges. Pia and Lynn have provided the answers and realistic expectations for the challenges that are inevitable for the child and the puppy.

We'll be putting this at the top of the ASPCA recommended reading list and await the inevitable increase of humanely raised puppies, and happily educated and empathetic children.

—Edwin Sayres Jr., President ASPCA

Introduction

"He is your friend, your partner, your defender, your dog.
You are his life, his love, his leader.
He will be yours, faithful and true, to the last beat of his heart.
You owe it to him to be worthy of such devotion."
—Unknown

Between the two of us, we have bred, raised, trained, and lived with a variety of dogs for over 20 years. In the early part of 2004, neither of us had a puppy or even a young dog in our homes; all of our dogs were adults. Then it happened. "Shall we get a puppy?" Pia asked her husband. Unbeknownst to Pia, Lynn was asking her husband the same question. We both thought about the empty crates in the basement, the carefree days with no concerns about open doors and missing dogs, housetraining, and the interrupted nights to take a puppy outside. Pia had concerns over the amount of time she could spend with a puppy, because of her work schedule and travel for speaking engagements around the world. Lynn's concerns were even greater—did she want to take on the responsibility of a puppy with two toddlers in the house? Would she have time to give the same care to this new puppy as her other dogs had received? Would either of us have the time?

Inevitably, our little bundles of cuteness danced into our lives (as puppies do!). Pia's a female; Lynn's a male. The puppies were everything we could hope for—fearless, joyous, curious, and confident. "Will this last?" we wondered. We reflected back on everything we learned with our prior puppies, and everything our training had taught us about the importance of early socialization and training. Even with the huge responsibility a puppy brings, we felt confident that we had the knowledge to raise our puppies correctly as part of our families. But, we started thinking, what about the majority of dog owners who are not trainers and animal behavior experts? Are they aware of the importance of puppy selection and how to pick a winner? Are parents aware of the importance of early rearing and how this may affect the relationship their puppy has with their children?

We realized that the resources that existed on the topic of raising puppies, especially raising puppies and children together, were quite limited. We decided to pool our talents and expertise to give you a complete guide to raising a happy, behaviorally healthy puppy. Going through the "puppy raising" process again ourselves gave even more urgency to our desire to bring this information to you.

We asked each other what message we wanted to get out to families with children and dogs. Little did we know that we had both been thinking about writing a book for many years, specifically on these topics. Pia's interest began 18 years ago, after adopting her rescue Golden Retriever, realizing that children and dogs require education about each other in order to live a harmonious life. Lynn began keeping notes 5 years ago while observing her dog's interactions when their first baby came home from the hospital. The research (and fun!) continued over the last few years to include observing her toddlers' interactions with their new puppy.

Millions of dog bites to children are reported each year; many more are not. How many people seek the help of professionals and how many quickly put blame on the dog? The dog is sent off to a shelter or even worse, sometimes put to sleep as a result. Could some of these bites have been prevented with a little education to help both canine and child learn how to better communicate with one another?

We are hoping that this book brings attention to the fact that parents must, early on, establish rules, boundaries, and training for both child and dog. We hope that it will help to educate parents as to how children and dogs should properly interact with one another and when to intervene in order to avoid problems. Above all, we hope to convey that dogs are dogs and children are children, and you must always supervise!

You will find this book to be a valuable resource whether you have a puppy, a young dog, or even an older dog; and whether you have children of your own, children who your dog sees on occasion, or you are expecting a child and have a dog currently in the home. We encourage you to read the entire book and then use it as a reference guide when you come across a problem or are unsure about your dog's behavior throughout the life of your new best friend.

"Whoever said you can't buy happiness forgot little puppies." —Gene Hill

Before You Get Your Puppy: What You Should Know

Chapter 1

Puppies: The First 12 Weeks of Life

Your goal as a new "puppy parent" should be to give your puppy the best possible start in life. It is essential that you provide your puppy with proper care, nurturing, and socialization during his first 16 weeks. The puppy's first few months are the most important months of his entire life, and they are crucial to his social development and future well-being.

The average puppy will learn more between the ages of 3 to 16 weeks than he will in his entire lifetime. What occurs during this critical period of development has an everlasting emotional and cognitive effect on the dog. Unfortunately, we only have control over a certain portion of this critical socialization period, since we typically do not get puppies until they are around 8 weeks old. It is important that you are aware of the developmental stages your puppy goes through, so that you can start off on the right foot. How the puppy spent his first 5 weeks of life is critical in laying the foundation for him to become a physically and behaviorally healthy dog.

Canine Development

Neonatal Period

Puppies are fairly helpless for the first 12 days of their lives. Their eyes and ears are not yet open and their motor capabilities are quite limited. They are basically deaf and blind, cannot regulate their own heat, or eliminate without stimulation. During this neonatal period, much of their time is spent nursing and sleeping. If puppies are handled and exposed to mild environmental stressors, it can have a positive impact on them in later years. On the other hand, pups left undisturbed or raised in isolation during this time can be emotionally reactive when they reach adulthood. You may not see visible signs until they reach adulthood (typically 2 to 3 years of age, depending upon the size and breed of the dog), because the signs are so subtle that the novice eye would not recognize them as a potential future problem. Some of these signs might be a dog who startles quickly from sudden movements or sounds (i.e., dropping a newspaper on the floor); a dog who vocalizes or appears to be "on guard" from every little noise; a dog who has a difficult time being left alone without being destructive, bordering on separation anxiety; or a dog who shies away from people and barks at other dogs.

Transitional Period

Pups go through what is called a transitional period somewhere between 12 and 21 days. During this time, they begin to develop their sensory and motor skills, typically between 18 to 19 days. Their eyes and ear canals open and they exhibit greater control over themselves. The puppies begin to walk unevenly, start to eat soft meals (since their teeth start to come in), and emerge into the world with an amplified amount of social and environmental stimulation. Even if they are warm and comfortable, vocalization will begin to take place when the pups are left in a new environment. Since their hearing is developing, a startle response develops to noises. Social behaviors begin with the dam and littermates. They also start to leave the "nest" or "den" to urinate and defecate.

Socialization Period

The socialization period starts at about 3 weeks of age and typically ends somewhere around 12 weeks. This is a very sensitive period in every dog's development. Furthermore, it is the optimal time for puppies to experience and learn about the world they will soon be challenged with, without becoming fearful.

The socialization period starts at about 3 weeks of age.

3 to 5 Weeks

Between 3 to 5 weeks, pups go through a preliminary socialization stage where a great deal of learning occurs. Much of this learning establishes a foundation for future behavior patterns (good and bad) that will be exhibited by the dog later in life. Breeders will see more signs of distress in the litter through vocalization. This may result in whimpering, whining, and sometimes what seems to be screaming. The pups also begin to play with their littermates through physical contact by using their mouths. They will bite, grab, shake, and hold each other. During play, if one pup bites too hard or takes hold of the skin or fur and grabs their littermate with force, the littermate will let out a loud high-pitched yelp, resulting in a sudden stop in play. The pause in play signals to the "aggressor" that his tenacity hurt. The "injured party" learns that yelping caused the unpleasant interaction to stop. The too-hard mouth play of one pup caused play to cease (a punishment). The yelping puppy also caused play to cease (a reward). Each puppy learned a valuable lesson through this interaction. The "biter" learned that play will cease if he continues

A great deal of learning goes on in the first few weeks.

to play with the same force. The "bitee" learned that a high-pitched yelp caused the teeth to be removed from her body and caused the pain to stop. However, unlike humans, dogs don't hold grudges and storm away insulted by what just occurred; they quickly begin playing again. The bolder pup will now bite a bit softer. He has learned to use his mouth carefully so the fun will continue. The other puppy learned to yelp when he felt threatened, afraid, or in pain.

Between three to five weeks a great deal of learning occurs.

How many people have quickly taken hold of a puppy and been surprised by a loud yelp? This was something the puppy learned during play. It serves as a safety cue, and it is critical for you to keep in mind. If your puppy yelps when your child is playing with, hugging, or squeezing him, he is trying to communicate with your child. His yelp should not be ignored.

During this time, there is also an increase in curiosity to inanimate or innocuous objects, and puppies need to begin exploring the world around them. Reputable breeders ensure that the puppies have time to explore in a safe manner. During the exploration time, pups must have the ability to escape if they become fearful. Studies have shown that during this period of time, if pups have been kept in cages or placed outdoors in cages with no means of escape, they will not develop a proper escape response. We often hear from owners after a dog-biting incident that the dog appeared to be fearful and could have backed away, but instead became rigid and bit the approaching child. This is probably because the dog never learned an escape response.

This is a time when the personality of the pup becomes more visible. The bold or assertive pups tend to start and end games, move further away from the litter to investigate without exhibiting fear, and show curiosity by batting at or attacking objects. More timid or cautious pups may follow their bold littermate, shy away from objects, or wait to see what happens as a result of the bolder puppy's investigation.

Which type makes a better pet for children? It is very difficult to say, since the pups will change from day to day and week to week during this stage. The bold pup might appear to be fearless one day and apprehensive the next and vice versa. Sometimes a bold pup might be perfect for certain children whose personalities are intrepid, and a quiet pup may be right for children who are quiet by nature. We like to match the personalities of the puppies and the children as closely as possible when we

Five-week-old litter of puppies.

evaluate puppies for families. Of course, if there is more than one child in the family, not every one will have the same personality. In that case, a puppy who seems to be well balanced would be the best choice.

5 Weeks

At approximately 5 weeks of age, the weaning process begins. Breeders typically do not interfere with this process, since the mother's snapping and growling at the pups for improper behavior is critical for their future well-being. The pups can learn a tremendous amount from their mother during this stage, about both people and dogs. If the dam's behavior to an approaching adult, child, or dog triggers a fear response in the puppies, they may become fearful of people and/or dogs later in life.

At 5 weeks, puppies learn a tremendous amount from their mother.

Insufficient socialization during this period can lead to many emotional problems in later years. Improperly socialized dogs may appear to be hyperactive, have less coping skills than other dogs, exhibit

Exposing puppies to the environment.

anxiety, fear or aggression, display compulsive behaviors (i.e., licking paws, spinning, chewing on themselves), and vocalize more than the average dog. When puppies are separated from the litter during this period, they may develop an intolerance of other dogs, and not be able to understand or recognize normal canine social behavior. If the pups are not socialized with people (especially children) during this time, they may become mistrustful later in life, since they have had little or no experience with them.

Many people wonder why a puppy who grew up in a household with children would be rambunctious with, or intolerant of, their children. The answer is simple—if the puppy's exposure to children was not positive and pleasant, the pup may grow up not enjoying interactions with them. Children's behaviors are quite different from the behaviors of adults. Children tend to see puppies more like playmates or toys, and their impulse control isn't as strong as ours. All of this can intimidate a puppy if you are not careful.

6 to 12 Weeks

The secondary socialization period occurs somewhere between 6 and 12 weeks of age, and the developmental period that appears to be the most influential is typically around 9 weeks of age. Even though the pups are more willing to investigate and approach new things during this time, they also exhibit more fear. As we've learned from the experts over the years, it is critical that puppies are provided with enough social contact so they learn to enjoy both people and dogs. Furthermore, the pup must have as much exposure to as many things in the environment as possible during this socialization period.

Whatever your pup experiences during this secondary socialization period will make a huge impact and remain with him for the rest of his life. Therefore, you will want to capitalize on this critically important time and set the patterns for a well-behaved dog. By 7 weeks, your puppy's brain is developed sufficiently to allow him to process what he needs to learn.

KEEP IN MIND

Begin Training Early

We brought our puppies home at 7 weeks of age and, by the end of the first week, their obedience training had begun. By 9 weeks, the pups traveled nicely in their crates in the car, visited relatives, had wonderful experiences at the veterinarian's office, and began meeting new canine friends of similar age. They were exposed to people of many cultures and took daily trips to public places (e.g., shoemaker shop, cleaners, farm stand, garden center, neighbor's barn, and several parks so they could get used to putting their feet into water, and more). We did this to ensure the pups would be well balanced and confident later in life.

Making sure your pup is socially developed is critical. A pup will not develop properly if his surroundings do not provide him with sufficient experiences. If you should come across some behavior in your puppy that concerns you, we recommend that you speak to a professional in the field. See the Appendix to learn more about what type of professional you may want to seek out and where to find one.

Juvenile Period

From approximately 12 weeks of age through sexual and behavioral maturity, the puppy enters the juvenile stage, or adolescent period (or as we like to call it "the teenage years"). Since this can be a very difficult time for

Make sure you have an understanding of what living with a puppy will be like.

you, the dog, and the children, we have dedicated an entire chapter to this topic. (See Chapter 11, The Juvenile Stage.)

What You Can Expect During the First 12 Weeks

Your puppy *will*:

- have accidents in the house, despite your best efforts to take him out every hour.
- wake up in the middle of the night, crying to be let out to relieve himself. She *cannot* physically hold it all night at this young age.
- chew your personal belongings (like shoes and clothing) if they are not kept out of sight or high enough where the puppy cannot reach them. He is not being spiteful! He is a puppy.
- play with your children's toys and possibly destroy them. Children must pick up after themselves since the puppy doesn't understand "yours," "mine," and "theirs."
- jump on your children, knock them over, bite at their clothing, hair, arms, and legs, causing your children to become angry, upset, or annoyed. He is simply reacting to their exuberant behavior.
- shred paper (your child's homework perhaps), take tissues from wastebaskets, chew on pencils, pens, or other items left on coffee tables, end tables, or your desk.
- take laundry from the laundry basket and possibly elicit chase games.
- attempt to jump up onto furniture and beds.

- chew on table legs, carpets, curtains, plants, and more. The puppy is having a good time—in his mind!
- probably tear apart his new bed that you purchased, as well as stuffed animals and other soft objects.
- find great joy in pulling sofa cushions and pillows off the sofa to play with and shred.
- put everything he can find into his mouth. It doesn't matter what it tastes like. If it gets your attention, it must be worthwhile.
- bite at and gnaw on your hands, arms, and feet. Like children, they go through a teething process and their gums are sore. Puppies use their mouths to play. Since they haven't learned the "play rules" yet, they are simply being puppies.

Now that you have a better understanding of what your puppy's first 12 weeks are like, you will want to make sure you select the right puppy for your family and lifestyle.

Chapter 2

Considerations When Selecting a Puppy

So, how do you know if you are ready to take on the responsibility of bringing a puppy into your household? Getting a puppy for a family with children should not be taken lightly. More important the new puppy venture will often be more than you anticipated if you don't research carefully. Take your time and wait to find the perfect pup for you and your family. *Never get a puppy on impulse*. It is easy to become smitten once you see the pup, even though your intent was to make an unemotional decision. If you feel sorry for the puppy because he was hiding in the corner, or you simply couldn't resist that cute little bundle of fur when he was put into your arms, you may be off to a bad start. Waiting for the right dog to come along will make it easier on you, as well as the rest of the family, in the long run. If you want to sail into the sunset with your new best friend, careful planning is required.

A Puppy for Your Child?

One of the biggest mistakes parents make is getting a puppy "for the children." Over and over again we hear, "It's Johnny's puppy—it is his responsibility." Children should not have this burden put upon them. Not only is it impractical, but unfair to both the child and the puppy. Puppies need consistency in their lives in order to function well, and the

If rules change from day to day, your puppy will become confused.

behavior of children is inconsistent. When the rules change from day to day and the boundaries are unclear, the puppy will become unruly and confused. When you force a puppy to guess what is expected of him, most puppies will do what pleases them. Who wouldn't? But can you blame the child for not establishing clear guidelines and following through? Or the puppy for not understanding right from wrong? No, both the puppy and child are being set up to fail in this circumstance. This certainly is not what we recommend to help develop a healthy relationship between dog and child.

Take a good look at your children's calendar. Is it busier than your own? Once the novelty of the new pup wears off, mom or dad will have an added responsibility. Will you have time to care for the pup? Many mothers and fathers in today's society work full or part time, as well as take care of the home and family. Very few of us have time to "stop and smell the roses" anymore. We rush from meeting to meeting, running errands in between.

Children also have enough pressures in their lives with schoolwork, extracurricular activities, chores, and friends. We know—we've been there. As children, we promised our parents that we would be involved in the feeding and care of the puppy, in addition to making our beds every morning, never fighting with our siblings again, improving our grades in school, and so on. Guess who ended up taking care of the puppy? Understand, there is nothing wrong with getting a puppy for the family; but please make sure that the adults in the home are prepared to take on the responsibility of raising her.

A Puppy for Your Other Dog?

The second mistake many people make is purchasing a puppy as a companion for their resident dog. While most dogs do enjoy the companionship of another dog, most dogs do not need to live with one. Again, take a good look at your lifestyle. If you are having a difficult time taking care of one dog (along with a family), and are feeling guilty for not having adequate time for the resident dog, then you certainly will not have time to care for two dogs.

More important, there is no guarantee that the two dogs will get along. For example, an elderly dog that is set in her ways may not appreciate the fact that you have surprised her with a "toddler" to care for. Imagine overwhelming your 87-year-old mother with an infant to care for simply because you thought she needed company. The energy level of a 9-year-old dog is not even close to that of a 10-week-old puppy. Once the puppy hits the juvenile stage, the elderly dog may dislike the puppy even more.

Some pet owners purchase a dog for their "feisty" dog (a dog that exhibits aggressive behavior toward people and/or other dogs) with the hope that the dog's aggressive behavior will change when she sees that the puppy is social and likes people and dogs. It will not. You may like certain folks, but just because you are friendly toward them doesn't mean your significant other will feel the same. When dogs do not get along with other dogs or children, the main reason is lack of proper socialization. Getting a new puppy will not help the resident dog learn to like others. The dog may eventually learn to like the puppy, but there are no guarantees.

Last, if you have little time to exercise your current dog, then avoid getting a puppy in hopes that the two dogs will exercise each other. While this wish may come true, you could end up with two out-of-control dogs, neither of whom listens to you. Your frustration level will increase, especially during morning hours when you are attempting to get the children ready for school and the dogs are outside enjoying the wonders of the world (and "Come" is not part of their vocabulary). They have each other and the great outdoors, so why listen to you? Dogs require constructive exercise; they do not self-exercise. While puppies can learn to play by themselves, they obviously don't have monitors to gage exactly how much exercise is enough for that day. Many people think the dog is getting sufficient exercise when he runs around the yard, chases after the children, or plays with another dog. He is not. Most dogs who run around the yard are simply getting rid of a small part of their pent-up energy. This does not fall into the category of constructive exercise and play.

Two puppies at once? That's one too many!

Two Puppies at Once?

The third mistake some people make is to purchase two puppies at one time, either from the same litter, or simply because they couldn't resist the second puppy sitting by himself in a cage. As any puppy owner will confess, raising one puppy can be extremely time consuming and exhausting. Unless you are home full time, have full-time help, and plenty of extra time on your hands, then we never recommend getting two puppies at once. Think of all the help a parent receives when twin babies come home. If it were easy, the additional help wouldn't be needed.

Housetraining issues become twice as difficult. Trying to keep track of when one puppy needs to go out is hard enough, but two puppies will not necessarily have to relieve themselves at the same time. Are you ready to take one out at 1:00 a.m. and the other at 3:00 a.m.? Even on the occasion when you get lucky and both will have to go at the same time, one of them may elicit a game of tag when the other is attempting to relieve himself, and the whole exercise is a wash. It's difficult enough to watch one puppy; think about watching two puppies, each going in different directions with shoes in their mouths!

Another reason why it's not a good idea to get two puppies at the same time is bonding time. This is a time when you will want to bond with your new puppy and spend as much time together as possible. Puppies, especially from the same litter, will bond with each other very quickly, long before they start to bond with you (unless you take them out separately and interact, train, and play with them one on one—do you have time for that?).

We don't recommend getting two puppies at once.

Last, many people don't think their two pups need socialization with other dogs since they have each other. This is not true. They will need individual socialization (without each other present) so they learn to get along with people and dogs on an individual basis, not as a team. Not many people in today's society have this kind of time in their lives, so think twice before making a mistake.

What Type of Puppy Is Right for You?

Puppies come in many different shapes and sizes. Now that you've decided to take on the adventure, there are many avenues to pursue. First of all, begin by developing a list of the desired traits that you are looking for in your new canine companion. To help you in making your selection, consider the traits and characteristics listed here:

- breed (purebred or mixed breed)
- size (small, medium, or large dog when the pup reaches adulthood)
- energy level (working breed with lots of energy or a couch potato type)
- coat (short- or long-coated dog; fur or hair)
- sex (male or female)

Breed

Purebred

If you are unsure as to what breed might be best, we suggest that you read about purebreds to see what type of dog would suit your family. You may also want to call a few breeders, visit dog shows, and talk to people who have the breed you are interested in, so you can learn more about their temperament, behaviors, and needs (e.g., high energy, requiring lots of exercise). Often, people admire unusual or uncommon dogs like our Belgian Tervuren because they look so attractive, but when they hear about the amount of exercise and training they need, many quickly cross them off the list. Research is important to avoid making hasty decisions. Avoid getting a pup simply because you like the looks or size, or the breed has suddenly become popular.

Are Certain Breeds Best for Kids?

Puppies and children can wind each other up like a top and before you know it, one of them is screaming for help. Even if you did your homework by selecting a dog from a list of breeds that you read were "good with kids," there still is no guarantee that they will get along. When we read the descriptions of dogs' temperaments and personality traits in breed books, the majority of them say "good with kids." Who can truly predict the future behavior of a dog or child? To say that certain breeds are great with kids is troublesome, because it gives people a false sense of security and the expectation that it will be easy.

Research is important when choosing a puppy.

In our area, the most popular breeds of dogs that families get are Golden Retrievers and Labrador Retrievers, simply because people have heard that these breeds are good with children. They think that the dog and child will require little or no supervision, and are shocked to find out that these breeds can and do bite (as all dogs will) if the situation calls for the dog to protect himself.

Many parents might avoid getting herding breeds, thinking that they will constantly chase after children, nipping at their heels. While this may be true in some cases, you can teach them otherwise. We both live with herding breeds (five between us), and all five get along beautifully with children. We credit our good breeders and ourselves for making sure the dogs started their training at a young age and were properly socialized with children. None of them nip at children's heels!

Breeders

If you decide on a particular breed of dog, there is some important information that you should be aware of before making the purchase. We recommend that you go to a professional reputable breeder. The list below will help you find one.

- **Get References.** The Internet can be a great resource for you on your search for a breeder. Remember, however, that anyone can develop a web site on just about anything. Dog sites are no different. Get as much information as you can about the breeder and obtain as many references as possible. Professional breeders rarely, if ever, advertise a litter in the newspaper, nor do they ever put signs up on highways or other local roadways. Many times the pups are spoken for before they even "hit the ground."

Breeder handling/training a 5-week-old puppy.

- **Health Issues.** Reputable professional breeders are concerned about the dam's (mother's) and sire's (father's) conformation, temperament, and much more. Both parents should be certified for sound hips (and elbows for large breeds), as well as having their eyes and heart checked. Many breeds are prone to thyroid disease, epilepsy, and cancer problems. You should ask the breeder if there are any known health problems in the last three generations of dogs. Having papers for your dog simply means that the dog's parents were both registered purebred dogs, and nothing more. These papers are not a health guarantee, or a guarantee as to the kind of dog your puppy will become.

- **Socialization.** A reputable professional breeder is aware of the critical socialization stages and what to do to ensure that the pups end up having good behavioral health.

- **Temperament.** A well-tempered dam will protect her litter for the first 2 to 3 weeks and thereafter permit people to handle the pups. Ask questions about the sire's and dam's temperaments, both with dogs and people. The dogs should be friendly and outgoing—they shouldn't be leery of you or exhibit any aggression. If the breeder makes a generalized statement like, "Don't think you're going to find a working dog who doesn't growl when someone comes to the home," be leery about what kind of socialization the pups may have received. We have owned working dogs for many years, and our dogs are friendly to all who enter our homes. Temperament of the sire and dam is passed down to the pups, and pups learn behaviors from their mother. If the mother growls at strangers, you can bet the pups are learning. If you have any doubts, go with your gut feeling. People have often told us that they were suspicious early on about their puppy's behavior and later realized that their suspicions were right.

- **Visit the Dam.** Professional breeders are filled with pride to show off their sires, dams, or other pups who may have been born from the line. If the breeder gives any excuse whatsoever about why you cannot visit with the litter or dam, we suggest that you look elsewhere. Be cautious about purchasing a puppy if the dam died during childbirth or the puppy was a singleton (single pup in the litter), especially if you have children. Although a reputable breeder will work diligently on getting the puppy socialized, other puppies or dams may not always be available. If the pup is raised without a mother or littermates, problems may develop later in life.

- **Out-of-State.** If you are getting a pup out-of-state and can't fly out to visit the site where the puppies are raised or to bring the pup home with you, your second option might be to pay for the breeder to fly out with the puppy, so the pup can travel in the cabin and not be shipped as cargo. Many people may not have this luxury and will need to have the puppy flown out in a crate; therefore, ask that the breeder acclimate the puppy to the travel crate well in advance. The pup should be taken away from the litter and put into the crate to sleep at night, so being taken away from the entire litter without any acclimation time doesn't traumatize the pup. Also, make sure the flight is direct and ask the breeder to wait to see that the crate is placed onto the right plane. Many web sites will give you advice on flying a dog.

- **Problems.** A responsible breeder will take the dog back at any age rather than see the dog given up. A reputable breeder shows interest in the pup and will want to stay in touch with you and answer any questions you might have. After all, you haven't purchased a sweater!

If you are unsure about which puppy in the litter is best for you and your family, by all means, get the breeder's advice. It is helpful if you come with a checklist of what you are looking for in an adult dog as well as details about your lifestyle. Reputable breeders carefully observe each puppy on an individual basis and will do their best to match the right puppy with your family. An exuberant, confident pup may not always be suitable for a family with four children. Neither would a timid one, so avoid selecting the quiet one in the corner. Pups, like children, should be playful, silly, and cuddly. If the puppy isn't making you laugh and your children aren't giggling, this is not the right puppy for you!

Rescue

You can also get a purebred dog from a breed-specific rescue group. These dogs are typically placed in foster homes until a permanent home can be found. These foster homes are typically those of breeders or knowledgeable people who have owned and loved the breed for many years. Many rescue groups work closely with shelters and will take purebred dogs from owners and shelters to avoid having them stay in a kennel-like environment. They typically take the dogs into their home and evaluate the dog's temperament in hopes of matching the dog up with new owners. While we have rescued many adult dogs, they do not come without some baggage. Make sure to ask a lot of questions about the dog's early life and why or how he came to be with the rescue organization. It is unusual for rescue groups to have puppies. Most of these groups have adult dogs.

Many people prefer to rescue or adopt dogs from shelters or rescue groups.

Mixed Breed

Many people prefer to rescue or adopt dogs from shelters or rescue groups, which for the most part will have mixed-breed dogs. You may try doing some research on a web site called Petfinder (www.petfinder.org), which lists various shelters across the country. Beware of sites that list all of their dogs as sweet, friendly, loving, and wonderful with children.

Here's what to look for at a rescue or shelter:

- Before visiting the shelter, do the same research as you did with breeders. Ask questions and obtain information about their return policy. A good shelter will accept any dog as a return after adoption. If the shelter only gives you a 30-day return policy, be concerned.

- It's important to learn about different breeds and their characteristics before you adopt a mixed breed. For example, if you have small, active children, a dog who is a mix of three different types of terrier breeds, for example, might not be the best choice.

- Once at the shelter, do not be afraid to ask questions about the puppy's background. Some key questions might be: *Where is the mother? Was the litter found or relinquished? Did the puppy come with his/her littermates or alone?* There will be times when the shelter doesn't have background information (e.g., what kind of dog gave birth to the litter). Many times they are simply making an educated guess about the mix of breeds in the puppy.

- Good shelters and rescue groups, like breeders, will ask you many questions about your family lifestyle. Don't become insulted if you feel that you are being interrogated. They are simply making every effort and attempt to match you with the right puppy to avoid future relinquishments.

- Ask what their criterion is for temperament testing litters of puppies or individual puppies. Many shelters test adult dogs before adopting them out. While no temperament test is foolproof, it will provide the staff with some idea about the pup's temperament, to help match the right puppy with your family. For example, a puppy who is exhibiting some guarding behaviors when he eats is probably not a good choice for a family with children. Some key questions to ask: *Does the puppy protect his bones, food, or objects? Does the puppy get along with other dogs? Has the puppy ever growled or shown his teeth for any reason? Does the puppy mind being picked up and held? If so, does the puppy quickly settle down or become agitated using his teeth to be released? Has the puppy ever bitten anyone? Can you easily take an object from the puppy's mouth, especially if the puppy feels the object is of high value? If not, what does the puppy do? What does the puppy do when you clip his nails? Does the puppy respond to training? How do you know if the puppy is good with children? Has the puppy exhibited fear during thunderstorms or other loud noises?*
- Ask about the shelter's support policy. If you are having trouble with your puppy, do they offer free services for behavioral counseling, or can they recommend an educated trainer or behaviorist in the area?

Size

An important consideration when trying to decide what type of puppy is right for you is the size that the puppy will be as an adult dog. Let's face it, puppies are adorable! At only 2 months old, even the largest of breeds are small, cuddly, and fluffy. Saint Bernard's fit this picture perfectly, but that small puppy will grow quite rapidly into an adult dog typically weighing over 100 pounds. Is that what you want?

Consider where you live—in an apartment or a house with a yard? How much room is there for a dog? Consider your lifestyle—are you an outdoor type that enjoys hiking,

Consider the size the puppy will be as an adult dog.

swimming, etc.? Do you often travel by air, and would like to take your dog with you? For most, this is easier with a small dog, since he can fly in the cabin of the plane with you under your seat. Cleaning up after your dog may also be a consideration for you—it's much easier to clean up after a 15-pound dog than it is a 120-pound dog, but your small 15-pound dog may not enjoy a walk on a cold, windy, snowy, wet evening. Before getting a dog, take all of these into consideration so you don't become frustrated later in your dog's life.

Small Dogs

These are some common reasons why people feel they would like a small dog:

1. They are more easily managed, since they don't have the weight and strength of a larger dog.
2. Inappropriate behaviors typically aren't as much of a nuisance in smaller dogs as opposed to larger dog (e.g., jumping on people, pulling on the leash).
3. They can travel much more easily and are more widely accepted in public places (easy to take on vacation, which saves on a kennel stay or pet sitter).
4. They are perfect for apartment and condo living, since their crates and beds are smaller.
5. They eat less than larger dogs do, so they are less expensive to feed.

And, here are some common *misconceptions* about small dogs:

1. Because of their weight and strength, they think the dog will be better with children. (*Any poorly socialized dog can have problems with children.*)
2. People won't mind a small dog jumping on them. (*Remember, not all people want to be jumped on or have a small dog in their laps when sitting on the sofa.*)
3. They do not need as much exercise as other dogs. (*Many small breeds are very active and require as much exercise, if not more, than larger dogs.*)
4. They do not require training. (*All dogs require training.*)

Consider the pros and cons of small or large dogs before making your decision.

Larger Dogs

Some people are drawn to larger dogs for the following reasons:

1. They think the weight and strength of larger dogs allows them to handle the antics of an active child, and that large dogs will more likely tolerate the roughhousing of children.
2. Families who enjoy outdoor living feel a larger dog would be better suited for outdoor activities (e.g., sailing, hiking, biking, jogging, etc.).
3. Many people enjoy playing games with their dog and feel a larger dog will be more likely to retrieve balls, catch Frisbees, etc.
4. They want a watchdog or a dog who will "look after their children."

These are some common *misconceptions* about larger dogs:

1. Large dogs are tougher and will therefore be more tolerant of children's antics. (*Just because a dog's weight and size might be suitable for handling the rough and physical antics of an active child, doesn't mean the dog will like it or will be gentle in return.*)

2. Large dogs won't mind the cold and rain. (*Many large dogs will not enjoy being outdoors in the cold and rain if you do not get them accustomed to it. Also, many large breeds have very thin coats of fur*.)
3. Large dogs like to play games with people. (*All dogs must be taught to retrieve and play with you; it will not necessarily come naturally*.)
4. Large dogs make good watchdogs. (*Just because a dog is medium to large in size does not mean he will make a good watchdog.*)

Coat Type

Dogs were bred with different types of fur (and hair) for specific reasons. For example, the sporting breeds tend to have an oilier coat so water repels off them easily. Each type of coat requires special care. The fur of a long-coated dog will probably require more brushing than that of a short-coated dog, but simply because your dog has a short coat doesn't mean the dog doesn't require bathing and brushing. (We brush our dogs on a daily basis, right before they go out. If you get into the habit, and teach the dog to stand still, this chore only takes a minute or so.) If you don't spend time brushing your long-coated dog, you run the risk of the dog getting mats, burs, and other discomforts. Short-coated dogs also require daily brushing to keep their coats shiny and skin clean. Dogs with both coat types will shed. With long-coated dogs, you will probably see fur looking like tumbleweeds in corners of your house, whereas a short-coated dog's fur tends to fly around and stick like pine needles. If you have allergies or cannot deal with dog fur or dander, many dogs have been bred with hair instead of fur. If someone suggests a certain breed to you because it is "nonallergenic," this refers to the type of coat (fur or hair) the dog has.

Sex

In most breeds, females are typically smaller in size than males. Both sexes are equally intelligent and trainable. Having lived with both males and females, we feel there is something special about both. It is really your personal preference. We do, however, encourage you to spay or neuter your dogs, regardless of the dog's sex. Approximately 8 million dogs are legally euthanized (put to sleep) each year in the United States because they are unwanted, discarded, or found astray. Spayed and neutered dogs have a much lower risk of developing health problems later in life. Spaying a female does not alter her personality, yet neutering a male can have many positive effects. Neutered males tend to lift their leg less and are less territorial, and it decreases their desire to roam. It does *not* make them less of a male!

Both sexes are equally intelligent and trainable.

Don't Settle!

After you have carefully considered all of the traits you want in your puppy, if the breeder or shelter doesn't have one who fits your needs and wants, avoid purchasing or adopting "just anything" because you want a puppy now. *Never settle!*

If you do find a puppy who may suit your needs, take your time during the visit. And, remember these few key points:

You might find your perfect match at a rescue or shelter.

- Look for a puppy who is friendly, lovable, and affect-ionate. The puppy should seek your attention by jumping up onto you and attempting to get you to play by using his mouth in a playful manner.
- Puppies should easily come to you when you kneel down and pat the

Testing sociability at 5 weeks of age.

floor. They should not avoid interacting with you—this is not a good start. Do *not* select the puppy if he is quivering, or hiding under a table or in a corner. While this puppy may be able to be socialized with some extra work, not many parents have the time for this type of puppy, and you may be setting yourself up for failure. Once again, we can't stress the importance of avoiding bringing home a puppy simply because you feel sorry for him.

• When you pick the puppy up, he should appear to be happy, not frightened or fearful. You should be able to easily pet and hold the puppy. Puppies should enjoy human contact. The puppy will probably be a bit mouthy (putting his mouth and teeth on your hands and arms) up until 6 months of age. However, the puppy should not be so mouthy to the point of puncturing your skin. The pup should not back away, duck, or act fearful. Be somewhat concerned if he "shakes you off" after you've touched him. This is a signal that he really doesn't like the contact, and it may only get worse with time.

• Make sure the pup enjoys the company of your children. If he is avoiding your children and leaning against you for help, ask to look at another puppy. He is already telling you he isn't comfortable with children. He may *never* get used to them. If your initial gut feeling is not good, say no. When your children are interacting with the puppy, they should each take turns so as not to overwhelm the puppy. You can get a better read on the puppy if the interaction is done one at a time.

- Look out for any aggressive behavior toward other dogs or people. If you attempt to take something from the puppy's mouth and he growls, this is not the puppy for you. If he growls or lunges at anyone, put him back right away. You are making a 10-to 15-year commitment to this puppy—you do not want to live the next 15 years with heartaches and headaches because the dog cannot socialize with people, children, and/or other dogs.

**When choosing
a puppy,
never settle!**

Now that you have decided on the type of puppy you will get, it's important to know how to prepare and what to expect when you bring him home, so the puppy is safe and remains healthy.

Chapter 3

Getting Ready for Your New Puppy

Now that you have selected your new puppy, you need to make sure that you, your family, and even your home and property are prepared for the new addition. If you have children, you may recall the excitement and commotion before the baby was born—preparing the baby's room, purchasing all of the necessary items needed for the proper care and feeding of an infant, and of course "baby-proofing" your house to be sure the little one would be as safe as possible. All of these preparations should be made for your new puppy as well.

Preparing Yourself

Taking on the responsibility of raising a puppy should not be taken lightly. Doing it right will require a great deal of your time. Lynn can attest that having two young toddlers and a 7-week-old-puppy in the house is a true test of patience, energy level, and commitment to all of them. Try to remember as you find yourself saying, "Good grief, the puppy needs to go out again?!" that your efforts teaching him the rules of living in your house and how to interact with people during these early months will reap rewards in the future. It does get easier.

Take a look at your current schedule. When are your blocks of free time? Do you have any? If not, what could be changed in your schedule to make time to take the puppy out to eliminate, take him for walks, play with him, and groom him? If you work full time and must leave the puppy home all day alone, consider having a friend, relative, neighbor, or a dog walker come to the house at least twice a day to take the puppy out to exercise, play, engage in human interaction, and, of course, eliminate. A midmorning (approximately 11 a.m.) and midafternoon (approximately 3 p.m.) potty break session is necessary.

The amount of exercise your puppy will need will depend on the breed you have chosen as well as his temperament. There are certain breeds and certain dogs in general that are typically more active and will require more exercise to tire them out and keep them out of trouble. Did you select one of these puppies? If so, be prepared to take the puppy out frequently. A tired puppy will make your life much easier.

You will need to spend a great deal of time supervising your children with the puppy.

Are you someone who likes to get a full, uninterrupted 8 hours of sleep each night? That is not likely to happen with a young puppy in the house. Expect to be getting up and going outside during the night when the puppy needs to go. Some young puppies can make it all night (really, 5 or 6 hours) without needing to eliminate. You may be lucky and find that your schedule is a last trip outside around 11:00 p.m. and then the puppy sleeps quietly until 5:00 a.m. Another puppy may need to go out at 3:00 a.m. Parents understand the importance of getting up to care for their infant when he wakes up many times during the night to be fed or because he is wet and needs to be changed. You will need to make this same commitment to your puppy. The puppy will ultimately make it through the night, and one day you will be back to getting a full night's sleep, but it takes time. You cannot stay in bed because you are tired and it's cold out, and ignore the fact that the puppy needs to go outside. If there are two adults in the house, try to get the other person involved in this routine, perhaps taking turns every other night letting the puppy out.

Another component of preparing yourself for the new puppy is recognizing that if you have children, you will need to spend a great deal of time supervising your children with the puppy. You may be accustomed to leaving your children in the living room playing while you are in the kitchen preparing dinner. Once the puppy is there, you will not be able to leave him in the living room alone with the children. You will either need to remain in the living room with them, or plan on bringing the puppy into the kitchen with you.

Remember that a puppy will need to go outside to eliminate, go for walks, and to play all year round in all types of weather. If you live in a region of the country where the winters are cold, you might choose not to go outside to play with your kids because of the temperature, but you cannot do that with the puppy. He needs to go out, even if the temperature is only 20°F or it is pouring rain. Your puppy must learn to go out in all types of weather. We cannot tell you how many times we have heard from dog owners that their dogs will not go out to eliminate when it is raining (which means that they will end up eliminating in the house instead). Go out with your puppy in the rain and snow and have some fun. You might want to invest in a good raincoat and all-weather footwear for yourself if you don't already have them. (Of course, if you have a small toy-breed puppy, you may need to paper train for a short period of time.)

Preparing Your Children

Time and time again we hear parents say, "we got the puppy for the kids." As we discussed in Chapter 2, this is a big mistake. Children, especially young children, are just not mature enough to be expected to provide the time and care that a young puppy requires. Even older, high school-age children who may be able to handle some of the feeding, walking, and some training, simply do not have the time. Once the excitement and novelty of the puppy wears off, they will go back to their old routines again, and the needs of the puppy will be forgotten.

Appropriate interaction between child and young pup.

Even though the children will not have primary care and responsibility for the puppy, no matter what their age, they do need to learn that there are rules for interacting with the puppy. It is your job to help teach them these rules. If the kids are old enough to understand and comprehend what you are saying, try discussing this list of rules with them before bringing the puppy home. For young children, we cannot stress enough the importance of constant supervision. We will repeat this statement throughout the book: *puppies and children should never be left alone together!*

These are the rules to discuss with and establish for your children before the puppy comes home.

Proper Handling

When a new puppy comes home, it is a very exciting time for everyone. All family members will want their chance to hold the puppy. We strongly suggest that your children understand that they will not be permitted to pick the puppy up at first. Please see Secton 3 for more details on how to properly interact with a puppy.

No Running, Screaming, or Chasing in the House

One suggestion that will help prevent a lot of problems later on is to enforce that the children run as little as possible when in the house. A running

Puppies and children should never be left alone together!

target is a big temptation for a puppy, and he will not be able to resist chasing it. Depending on the type of puppy and his temperament, he may try to end the chase game by catching your children and stopping them by using his mouth. Having dogs and toddlers in your house, we recommend establishing a "no running in the house" rule. Running is something that is done outside. If your children or the dogs start running or playing rambunctiously, it is a sign that they have too much pent-up energy, so out they should all go to play! It makes life in the house so much easier to manage.

Teach your children not to play in your puppy's crate.

The Puppy's Crate Is Not a Fort or Dollhouse

We recommend that you use a crate for your puppy for housetraining purposes and as a place of confinement when you cannot watch him. If possible, purchase a crate before your puppy comes home and work with your children on establishing "the crate is off limits" rule. A crate is a fascinating place for young children. They are always interested in crawling inside, and even shutting themselves in. It is important to teach the children that the crate is for the puppy only and that they do not belong in there. Your puppy needs a place where he can feel safe and escape the excitement and commotion of your busy lives.

Never Open the Door to Let the Puppy Out of the House

This may sound obvious to us as adults, but young children will see you going through a routine every day of opening the door to take the puppy out, and they may decide at some point to do the same. Your children are watching your every move but may not be capable of understanding when and why you are doing this. They may attempt to mimic this behavior. This could be disastrous, especially if you do not have a fenced yard. Again, supervision is your key to success. Tell your children that when the puppy comes home, they must never open the door to let the puppy outside without your permission. If the children are young, they probably do not like being outside alone, and you can explain that the puppy will feel the same way. It is important that you teach them to always ask an adult before opening the door.

KEEP IN MIND

Letting the Dogs Out

The morning routine at Lynn's house is the same every day. She gets up around 6:30 a.m., throws on some clothes, and takes the dogs out to eliminate; then it's back in the house for breakfast. The kids are usually up at that point and will come outside with her or wait by the back door in bad weather. They know the routine. One morning, Lynn woke up and walked across her bedroom preparing to go downstairs. When she glanced out the window, she did a double-take, thinking she saw two black streaks (her dogs) moving across the yard. Luckily, her puppy was still in his crate in the bedroom. Lynn knew she had not let the other dogs out, and her husband had already left for work. The culprit soon showed herself—Lynn's 2-year-old daughter came into the bedroom. When asked if she had let the dogs out, she said with a very big, proud smile on her face, "Yes Mommy!" She figured that she would take care of the morning routine on her own—after all, why not, she knew what to do.

Remember, your children are not bad for doing some of these things. They are just trying to imitate you and to help you out!

They Should Not Take Matters into Their Own Hands

A simple rule to help prevent confrontations between your children and your puppy is to teach the children to come and get you if they feel there is a problem with the puppy, or if they are upset about something the puppy is doing. It is a much better course of action than allowing the children to take matters into their own hands. (You might want to then reprimand yourself for leaving them alone unsupervised in the first place!)

Let your puppy eat in peace.

Let the Puppy Eat

Children are fascinated by a puppy munching on his food. Young toddlers may want to get down on the floor with the puppy and may put their hands right in the food bowl. The children must understand that the puppy needs a chance to eat his meals in peace.

Preparing for Your Puppy's Health Care

You will need to find a veterinarian who will help you in providing proper medical care for the life of your dog. Talk to your friends and neighbors who have pets about the veterinarians in your local area. Go to the veterinarians' offices to meet them. Is the office staff friendly? Is the office clean? What is the cost of an office visit?

Select a veterinarian who is within a reasonable driving distance from your house in case you need to get there quickly in an emergency, and one that you feel comfortable talking to—you may be there often, at least in the first few months. If your veterinarian does not have 24-hour services, make sure you are aware of the closest 24-hour emergency veterinary clinic to your home.

Try not to wait until the last minute on this one. We highly recommend taking your puppy to a veterinarian for a checkup as soon as possible after bringing him home—even if you have been told that he is current on his vaccinations. It is important to know right away whether or not there are any signs of medical problems with your puppy. Many breeders, pet stores, and shelters require that you take the puppy for a full checkup within a specific period of time after taking him home. It is best for you and the puppy.

Puppies Must Have Routine Health Checkups

To ensure that your puppy maintains good health, your pup will be required to go through a series of inoculations to protect him from serious diseases. Vaccination procedures vary slightly from one clinic to the next, especially in different parts of the country, but you should be prepared to make several trips to the veterinarian in the first few months of your puppy's life. After that, an annual visit will be all that is needed, unless there are other health problems.

Parasites are also a concern, especially when the pup is young. Therefore, your veterinarian will want to routinely check your puppy's stool to rule out internal parasites. Once your pup is older, you will need to have the stool checked once a year. There are also external parasites that can cause your puppy to become ill, such as ticks and fleas. Lyme disease, caused by the bite of a deer tick, is very common in many areas of the country and can be deadly. Therefore, it is important to discuss preventative measures with your veterinarian.

Puppies Require Good Nutritional Diets

You make every effort to ensure that your child eats a well-balanced meal three times a day. Puppies require the same. Until they are 6 months of age, puppies should eat three meals a day. Depending on where you bought or adopted your puppy, you were probably sent home with some dry kibble that the

Until they are 6 months of age, puppies should eat three meals a day.

puppy has been accustomed to eating. You can continue to feed that kind or switch to another brand. There are many products on the market that are healthy for your puppy—what you feed your puppy is up to you. We prefer the holistic approach since the food products used are wholesome, fresh, organic, and free of disease. There are many natural dry dog foods as well as a variety of homemade versions for sale, or you can even home-cook meals for your puppy. Please check with your veterinarian if you decide to take the homemade route (unless you are educated in canine nutrition). If you feed your puppy a poor diet, the pup can become overweight and unhealthy. Avoid feeding fatty foods or leftovers that include heavy gravies.

You will want to check your puppy's stool to be sure that it is formed and solid. A runny, loose stool can be an indication that the food you are feeding is not the best type or variety for your puppy. Some puppies have more sensitive digestive systems than others, or even allergies to certain types of food, and may need to be put on special diets. If you have any question about whether or not the type of food you are feeding is right for your puppy, please see your veterinarian.

Preparing Your House

Now you and your family are ready for the puppy, but what about your house? It is time now to take a close look at the environment where your new puppy will live.

Puppy-Proof Your Home

Ideally, you should try to puppy-proof your home, which might involve changing your normal routine or that of your family members. Do you typically kick your shoes off by the door when you come home and then leave them there? Your shoes can be a great source of fun for your puppy—they are fun to play keep away with, because everyone in the house gets very excited and starts chasing the puppy whenever he has them. Most shoes are also made of a material that offers great chewing pleasure. You will need to change your routine by putting your shoes in a closet, or somewhere else where the puppy cannot get to them. When evaluating your home environment, always ask yourself, "How can I set my puppy up for success?" If your infant child was constantly crawling over to your shoes and putting them in her mouth, you would make sure that those shoes were put somewhere that the infant could not reach. Do the same for your puppy.

As we mentioned earlier in this chapter, your puppy will be going outside in all kinds of weather conditions. Are you prepared to take care of a potentially soaking-wet dirty puppy who has just come in from the rain? Start saving up those old bath and hand towels—they make great towels to dry off your puppy. Keep a few near the door where your puppy will be going in and out of most often. Spread one on the floor for him to walk on as he comes in, which will help clean the mud off his feet, and keep another to use for drying and wiping off any dirt. Yes, it will take a few extra minutes of your time on those rainy days, but it is a lot better than the frustration you will feel if the puppy runs through your entire house wet and muddy, ruining your good rugs. If you begin this process early on, your puppy will get used to waiting at the door to have his feet wiped and not mind the process. Our dogs even enjoy it.

You should try to puppy-proof your home.

Your Furniture

You should decide now whether or not you will be allowing your puppy on your furniture. Think about the size your puppy will be when full grown. Most people do not mind having their cute little fuzzy puppy snuggling on their laps with them while they are sitting on the sofa. Most young puppies do not shed, or at least very little and, of course, they are still quite small. Will you want your 80-pound, full-grown dog taking up half the couch, and leaving piles of dog hair woven into the fabric of your sofa? The choice is yours. The same goes for your bed or any other furniture in your home. Your puppy needs consistent rules in order to figure out how to live in your house with you. It is difficult for a puppy to understand that he is allowed on the furniture most of the time, but then when he is wet from being out in the rain and jumps up on the sofa, you get angry at him for doing so. He thinks he is allowed there and is confused by your actions. It is easiest to make an on-or-off rule from the moment the puppy comes home. Your puppy does not need to be on the furniture to be comfortable; he is perfectly fine lying on the floor or carpet. You can also provide a dog bed for him to lie on. If you decide that your puppy (and soon to be full-grown dog) will be allowed access to your furniture, teach him that he may only get up there when invited by you and, even more important, that he must get off

Your puppy won't know the difference between his toys and your child's toys.

when told. If at any time your puppy gives you a hard time about getting off of your sofa or bed (refusing to move, perhaps even grumbling or growling), you should immediately cut off all furniture access from that point forward. The furniture is not his—it is yours, and he can keep the furniture privilege provided he abides by your rules.

Stuff All Over the Floor

Take a look at the items that are normally found on the floors in your home. If you have small children, chances are there are toys left here and there on the floors throughout the house (we've already talked about your shoes and the need to put them away). Young puppies are very curious and very playful. They do not understand that these items are not theirs and should not be picked up or chewed on by their sharp teeth. If you find yourself constantly retrieving stolen items from your puppy's mouth, it might help you to pick a room where the children's toys can be on the floor and limit the puppy's access to that room. Of course, you will have to get your children to help you with this one. Children will learn quickly to put their toys away once the puppy's sharp teeth destroy a valued toy. What about magazines or newspapers—are they easily accessible for the puppy to grab? In his mind, they are great fun to shred.

Set your puppy up for success!

Take a good look around your home—the floors and other easily accessible areas like coffee tables, chairs, the fireplace—and realize that you might have to move or put things away temporarily while the puppy is still young. We'll say it again: *Set your puppy up for success!*

The Bathroom

The bathrooms in your home are very interesting places to young puppies. Is the water in the toilet bowl another drinking bowl? They sometimes think so. Paper is a fun item for puppies to play with and shred, so make sure that your puppy does not get hold of your toilet paper roll. We've known puppies who have grabbed on to the toilet paper roll and run through their house with it—what fun! The bathroom garbage is also very accessible, since it is usually a small, low wastebasket with more fun stuff in it like tissues, disposable razors, etc. If your puppy is constantly sneaking off into the bathroom, help set him up for success by keeping the door shut. Of course, the main thing to remember is that your puppy should not have the opportunity to roam around the house and go into different rooms unless you are with him.

The Kitchen

What a wonderful place the kitchen is—filled with lots of food and interesting scents. Do you typically leave food out on your kitchen table or counters? This is such a temptation for your young puppy. He may be too small at first to reach the table top or counter, but eventually he will be tall enough, or will figure out a way to get up there. Again, supervision is the key to success. If the puppy is in the kitchen, you should be there as well. If you are using the kitchen to confine him once he is old enough to no longer need the crate, and he will be left there alone, make sure you have not left any food out—not even a crumb. Where is your kitchen garbage can? Is it out on the kitchen floor, or is it hidden in a cabinet? An unsupervised puppy will eventually get into a garbage can if he can, especially the kitchen garbage, which is filled with food scraps. Do not give him the opportunity to learn that this is an item worth dumping over.

Supervision is critical with a puppy— some plants are poisonous.

Plants

Be aware that the plants in your home can be very interesting to your puppy. He will sometimes investigate by pulling off leaves and even eating them. He may also be more interested in the dirt in the planter, rather than the plant itself. Are you aware that many common houseplants can be toxic to dogs? (You can check The National Animal Poison Control Center at www.napcc.aspca.org for more information.) You do not want your plants ruined, dirt all over the floor, or worse, a sick puppy. One simple key to success for all of these items is supervision—keep the puppy with you at all times and you will know what he is doing or, more important, what he is about to do so that you can stop him in the act.

Preparing To Leave Your Puppy Home Alone

There will be times when you will need to leave the puppy home alone. This will be easier for some puppies than it will be for others. Dogs are very social animals and enjoy the company of you and your family. It is often difficult for them to transition from having the company of a person all the time, to suddenly being left alone for a few hours. You will want to start to prepare your puppy for this transition as soon as he comes home.

When you need to leave your puppy alone, it is recommended that you put him in his crate. He will be safe in the crate; you can control what he has access to by giving him some water and an appropriate chew toy, and you'll know that your house will be safe. Make sure you take your puppy out for a good exercise session and to eliminate just before you are ready to leave. If the puppy is tired and content, he will be more likely to settle into his crate for a nap and not mind, or maybe even notice, that you have left the house. A little planning on your part, and spending a few extra minutes exercising the puppy, will go a long way.

Start off by leaving him alone for short periods of time; maybe 30 minutes to 1 hour while you go to the store. It is important that when you return home, you do not make a big deal about the fact that you are back. You do not want the puppy to think that the fact that you have arrived is the best thing that ever happened, because he'll start to think that when you are gone it's the worst. Simply come into the house and, when you are ready, go over to the crate calmly and quietly and let the puppy out. Talk to him in an unexcited, unemotional voice and bring him outside immediately to relieve himself. If he did well, you can slowly build the amount of time that you leave him alone, perhaps over a period of several weeks.

Preparing Your Yard

If you live in an apartment or townhouse with no yard you won't need to worry about this point, but for those of you who have yards for your puppies to roam in, we urge you to pay close attention to this section.

To Fence or Not To Fence?

This is a big decision, and one that most people make after getting the puppy home, not before. Many homeowners may have restrictions on the type or height of fencing that is allowed, based on where you live. Or perhaps you cannot put up fencing at all. Again, we go back to the importance of the planning stages and thinking about the type of dog you will be getting, and whether or not your yard environment is suitable for that dog. Good sturdy fencing of the proper height for your dog is a safe means of providing a restricted, confined outdoor area for your dog (by safe we mean that the dog cannot run away and other dogs cannot come on to your property to bother your dog).

For those who cannot or choose not to fence their yards with traditional fencing, there is the electric fence option. The electric fence consists of a series of transmitters buried around the perimeter of your property and a special collar your dog wears that causes him to receive an electric shock if he gets too close to the "fence line." Electric fencing for dogs has become very popular in more congested suburban areas. There are pros and cons to this type of fencing.

Pros:

- Your property maintains the same look it always had.
- Your puppy is kept in the yard so long as he is wearing the collar provided by the electric fence manufacturer.

Cons:

- The neighborhood dogs or other animals are not restricted from entering your yard and bothering with or even attacking your puppy.
- It only works if the puppy is wearing the special collar.
- It is a piece of electronic equipment that can malfunction. A dog may leave his yard because the collar stopped functioning and the dog did not receive a shock. Or, we know of a case where the dog was shocked continuously no matter where he was in the yard because of a malfunction in the equipment. This caused the dog to tremble in fear of going outside.
- Some dogs who enjoy chasing animals and/or people will "take the shock" in order to leave the area, yet not want to come back through.

If you decide to take the electronic fence route, then our suggestion would be not to train the puppy to the fence until he is older. This is just our opinion—we simply feel that putting an electronic collar on a young puppy can cause undue stress and have a negative impact on the dog later in life.

This is an example of a safe outdoor kennel run.

A Dog Run or a Tie Out?

These are two more options for containing or restraining your puppy when out in the yard. A dog run is a small fenced area, often with a doghouse where the dog can be safely confined, yet still be outside. If you do not want to fence in your whole yard, but want a small fenced area to keep your dog in outdoors, this may be the best option for you.

Pros:
- You can be outside and not worry about the dog.
- You can use it as a place for your dog to relieve himself and save your grass area.

Cons:
- The dog may spend a good deal of time barking if left out alone.
- Someone can enter your property and take your puppy.
- Your dog can dig underneath it and escape (as is the case with most fences).

Another option to fencing is to "tie the dog out"—tying a rope or line to your dog's collar that is connected to a stake in the ground. *We do not recommend ever tying a dog out*. This option is worse than the electric fence, since he will be more at the mercy of the neighborhood dogs—tied and unable to escape a stray dog or other animals coming toward him. We have heard many nightmare stories about tie outs. Dogs have wrapped themselves around trees and choked to death, broken limbs, chewed through the ropes or lines to free themselves, and run away. Behavioral problems can also occur, with the once friendly puppy becoming territorial and lunging and barking at everything that goes by.

We do not recommend ever tying a dog out.

54

C A S E   S T U D Y

Don't Tie Your Puppy Out

After much discussion, a neighborhood family with three young children decided to get a Golden Retriever puppy. Every day the adorable puppy was outside in the yard connected to a tie-out like the ones described above. No one was with him, he had no toys, bones, or anything else out there with him to occupy his time. Day after day, no matter what time of day it was, he seemed to be there. An adult was home all day, yet the puppy was tied outside. Why? This seemingly friendly puppy with a lot of potential could end up with unwanted behavior problems because of this daily "tie-out" routine. Discussions with the owner (we had to ask!) revealed that the puppy would start to get too rambunctious in the house (due to lack of exercise) and the adult who was home could not or did not want to deal with it, and therefore put the puppy out. This is an example of a family who was *not* ready to make the commitment to care for a puppy.

Using the Fence as a Babysitter?

This is not, we repeat, not appropriate. The type of fencing that you use, if you decide to get any at all, will not matter that much provided you are outside with your puppy whenever he is out there. This cannot be stressed enough—the number one rule should be: *when the puppy is outside, so are you.* We find that important point is often very difficult to get across to most dog owners. We hear, "I got the fencing so that I could let the puppy out for a while so I can do other things," or, "The puppy needs fresh air and loves it outside." Would you let your 1- to 3-year-old toddler out in the yard alone with no adult supervision? We think not! Be very careful that you do not give your puppy too much freedom or time alone without you.

Let's say you have a fenced yard, whether traditional fencing or electric. Initially, a new puppy, when left outside on his own, may not do much.

Never leave your puppy outdoors unattended. She will find ways to entertain herself.

As time goes on, he will start to explore more areas of the yard. Is your yard a safe place for your puppy? What items can be found in your yard that could pose a health risk to your puppy if he decides to take a bite out of them? What do you value in your yard that your puppy might destroy if left unattended?

Many people let the puppy out in the yard so that he will get some exercise. Dogs will rarely exercise themselves. They might go running out the door with some initial excitement, but that usually wears off quickly, and now they are just wandering and looking for something interesting to do. Chances are, the "interesting thing" that they will choose is probably not something of which you would approve (e.g., digging holes, eating your plants, chewing rocks, chewing the garden hose, or digging up the garden). If you are outside with your puppy and one of these undesired behaviors starts up, you can stop it immediately, letting your puppy know that you do not approve of the hole digging or hose chewing. If left alone, these things can become a fun pastime for your puppy, and will be much more difficult habits to get rid of later on in life.

Even worse than simply destroying your lawn and garden, a puppy left alone in a yard can develop a number of other unwanted behaviors. You may live in an area where people and dogs are often walking by your property. Since your puppy is probably bored outside by himself, this activity going on beyond the fence boundaries may really excite him. He starts off by fence running (racing back and forth along the fence line in an excited fashion). The fence running could then become paired up with excited and uncontrollable barking. Not only is this annoying for you and your neighbors, but it is not at all healthy for your puppy to get himself that aroused and worked up. After a few months, you may try to go out to stop your puppy while he is doing this and, as you reach to grab him in mid-run, he turns and snaps at you, or bites you! Even worse, if your children are out playing and get in the way of the fence running, he may knock them over, or redirect his frustration at an innocent child. Perhaps there is a neighbor dog just on the other side of your fence who might not be particularly friendly with dogs. As your puppy gets older, he may begin fence fighting with the neighbor's dog. What started off as an innocent behavior has turned into *your* nightmare.

The number one rule should be: When the puppy is outside, so are you.

Last, and very simply, a puppy left alone outside is *not* interacting with you. When our puppies are outside, we are with them every minute, and you must make every effort possible to do the same.

Lynn has a fenced backyard; Pia does not. In both cases, our puppies were with us no matter where we went in our yards. We made sure that we were a part of all the fun that they had outside, and taught them to look to us for their fun, not elsewhere. In Lynn's case, she also made it a point to periodically take her puppy into her unfenced front yard to play. She wanted him to learn to simply stick with her no matter where they were, fence or no fence. In Pia's case, since she lives on a farm with wide-open wheat fields and wooded areas on three sides, she spent every morning and evening walking the perimeters of the property, hiking the trails, and spent 2 hours a day on recall work (teaching her puppy to "come") to ensure that the puppy understood the boundaries, always knew how to get home, and focused her attention on Pia rather than chasing wildlife. What we both did was spend time with the puppies, developing a strong bond and good leadership. Because of all the time and effort we put in during the early months, we now have adolescent dogs who prefer to be with us rather than running off, even off-leash on a hike, or at a park.

CASE STUDY

Too Much Freedom Is Not a Good Thing

A couple came to us who had several acres of property fenced in with electric fencing and a doggy-door in the back door of the house so that their dog could go in and out as needed. This dog would roam alone, doing whatever she liked during the day, and would come back at meal times and to sleep in their bed at night. She did enjoy the company of her owners, but she did not *need* them. The complaint from the owners was that when they attempted to go for a hike with the dog, she would not listen to them and almost never came when they called her. Furthermore, the dog had little or no interest in playing with the owners, since her primary fun was chasing wildlife. Why chase a ball or Frisbee? Those games were much too easy for this sporty little dog and not nearly as fun as a deer that keeps running. The dog learned that outside was a place where she did her own thing, had a good time doing it, and the owners were not a part of that good time. And because it had gone on for so long, it was a way of life for her.

Preparing Your Car

Just as you prepare your car for the arrival of a new baby by purchasing an infant car seat, you should prepare the car for your new puppy as well. How big will your puppy be as an adult dog? What type of vehicle do you have? Is there enough room for your puppy, once he is fully grown, to be able to lie down in your car, preferably in a crate? We have heard many people say that they ended up buying a new car for their dog so they could properly transport them. (Hey, we've done it too!)

The safest way for a puppy or adult dog to be transported in a vehicle is in a dog crate. The puppy is protected in case of an accident, and is also prevented from causing an accident by distracting you or bumping your arm while you are driving. Dogs who are roaming loose in a car can easily be thrown from the vehicle or into the windshield, even in a minor fender-bender. Although a small puppy crate in the car may work fine for you during the first few months, you will need to start thinking about how big your puppy will be as an adult. Will a crate that is big enough for your adult dog fit in your car? Keep in mind that a crate for the car only needs to be big enough for the dog to stand up, turn around, and lie down. It does not need to be as big as the crate in the house that you use for housetraining. If you cannot fit a crate in the car, then consider using a seatbelt harness for dogs.

The safest way to transport your dog is in a crate.

Not only is it best for the puppy to be crated or secured with a seatbelt in the car for his own safety, but it is also the best way to protect your car from your puppy. If your puppy is loose in the car, then it is likely that the interior of your car will be damaged in some way because of something that the puppy does. Are you prepared to clean up after him if he has an accident? Like some children, puppies can get carsick. If he does get sick and vomits in the car, it would be a lot easier to clean up if it happens in a crate rather than on the seat of the car. There will also likely be times when the puppy or adult dog will get into the car when wet, muddy, or dirty. Are you prepared to have wet, dirty seats? What type of coat does your puppy have? Are you prepared to have his fur all over the car seats if he is loose? What about dealing with his strong desire to chew? If he is confined in a crate, then he cannot chew on parts of the car. If he is not confined while you are driving, he could be munching away on the back seat, and you will have a nice big

The safest way for a puppy or adult dog to be transported in a vehicle is in a dog crate.

hole somewhere or a seatbelt that's been chewed in half. It could also be dangerous for him, depending on what he is chewing and potentially swallowing. Instead of getting angry at your puppy for dirtying your car, help to set him up for success by using a crate or seatbelt harness. This will keep him safe and the car clean.

If your puppy will travel long distances or simply spend a lot of time in the car, it is a good idea to keep a water bowl, water bottle/jug, towel, and possibly an extra leash and collar in the car in case you need them.

Preparing for Your Vacation

Have you considered what you will do with your puppy when you and your family are away on vacation? This is an important consideration, and one that you should research now, rather than waiting until 2 weeks before you are leaving. You would not leave your children with a babysitter you never met, or send them away to a camp that you knew nothing about; so make sure that the person who will be watching your puppy or the place where you are taking him to will give the best care possible. You have a number of options.

You could decide to take your puppy to a kennel. Boarding kennels vary greatly as to how they look and the services they provide. Go to the kennel and ask for a tour—if they will not give you a tour, then do not even consider leaving your puppy there. Is it clean? Are the people friendly? How does the cost compare to other local kennels? Is your puppy accustomed to a lot of running and playtime in the yard? Try to find a kennel that will do that for him, rather than having him confined in a dog run for the week.

You might take your puppy to a trusted friend or family member's house, or hire a dog walker or pet sitter to come to your house several times per day, or even live in your home while you are away. Interview the dog walker or pet sitter and ask for references. Have them meet your puppy. How do they interact with your puppy? Does the puppy seem to like the person?

Find out if the pet sitter works alone, or if they have other people helping them—make sure you've met the person who will actually be coming to your house. Also, keep in mind that depending on where you are going and what you are doing on your vacation, many hotels will allow dogs in the rooms. If you don't think you can part with your new addition for a whole week, consider a vacation where he can go along!

Consider a vacation where your puppy can go along.

Items Your Puppy Will Need

There are a number of items that you will need to acquire, either before bringing your puppy home or immediately after, which will aid you in properly caring for your puppy. Here are some of the most important ones, so you do not find yourself without a puppy necessity.

Crates

The best type of crate for the house is generally one made of metal (wire-cage type). It cannot be chewed, is quite secure, provides good airflow, and the puppy can easily see out all sides. The crate for the car can be the same type, or you might want to consider a foldable crate. They are lightweight and can be easily carried and stored when not needed. You can find either type online or at your local pet store. You will probably want at least one crate to keep in your home, and another for the car, especially if your puppy will frequently travel in the car. You can certainly get by with only one crate if you do not mind moving it from the house to the car when needed.

Food

Your puppy needs a nutritious diet. There are many types of dog food on the market: dry kibble, canned, and raw diet (frozen or fresh). The type of food your dog will eat is ultimately your decision, but do your research to find nutritious food for your puppy.

A simple buckle-type collar is ideal for puppies.

Food and Water Bowls

You will need at least two dog bowls—one for food and the other for water. Stainless steel or ceramic are your best bets—plastic bowls can cause chin dermatitis in some dogs.

You may want to consider a weighted or non-tip bowl to use as your puppy's water bowl. The water bowl can be a great source of fun for many puppies, and it is best to have a bowl that the puppy cannot tip over. You may also want to keep a water bowl in the car if your puppy will spend a lot of time there. Many types of collapsible water bowls are on the market that are very convenient for storing in the car.

Collar and Leash

Your puppy will need a collar and leash. Our recommendation for a leash is to use one that is approximately 6 feet in length, made out of leather or nylon. We both prefer leather leashes because they are softer and easier to handle than other materials; however, you may want to wait until your puppy learns to walk properly on leash (and not to chew on it), before investing in an expensive leather leash.

The type of collar you use is your decision. There are many types from which to choose—our preference for young puppies is a simple buckle-type collar. It should fit just snugly enough so that you couldn't easily pull it over the puppy's head while buckled. You do not want it so loose that the puppy can back out of it, but not so tight that it would be uncomfortable. Most buckle collars are made of leather or nylon material, and your puppy's identification tags can be placed on his collar. There are also buckle-type collars called martingale collars that tighten slightly if the puppy pulls. If you decide to use this type, we recommend that it be properly fitted on your puppy by someone familiar with the equipment (such as your puppy's trainer). As your puppy gets older and stronger, you may need a harness or halter that will help you to walk and control a strong, pulling dog.

We *never* recommend using a choke collar. We feel they are dangerous pieces of equipment. If left on your puppy, his ID tags can get caught on things and, as the puppy tries to free himself, he could choke to death. Also, if the ring of the choke collar gets caught on a piece of furniture, falls between the slats of the deck, or gets caught on shrubs, your puppy may pull and possibly choke himself. If your puppy is a dedicated puller when on-lead, this collar is putting quite a bit of pressure on the pup's trachea, which may do severe damage. If you plan on showing your puppy, then this type of collar may be used for the show ring, and then removed when showing or show training is completed. All collars should be removed when the puppy is in his crate and unsupervised.

Toys for Play

You will want to teach your puppy to play with you using a variety of toys. There are toys for playing tug, toys that squeak and make noise, and toys for throwing, fetching, and chasing. You might choose a Frisbee or a ball to play with. Remember, your dog may not be a natural at retrieving a thrown object, so find something he does like to play with, and have fun with that.

Toys or Bones for Chewing

Most puppies are chewing machines. They need to chew, so it's up to you to provide appropriate chew toys or bones for them. If not, they will find something inappropriate to chew on, like the kid's toys, your shoes, or the furniture. If your puppy is going to be in his crate for a long period

"I love my bed!"

of time, it will help him to have an appropriate chew toy to safely pass the time. Please see Chapter 12 for more information on chew toys and bones.

Grooming Items

The specific grooming items you need will depend on the type of puppy you have and the specific grooming needs of his coat. Below is a list of basic grooming items that are required for most puppies:
- Nail clippers and styptic powder
- Brush
- Comb
- Shedding blade
- Scissors
- Shampoo for puppies
- Soft toothbrush and doggy toothpaste

Dog Bed

A dog bed is a nice item to have for any size dog. They come in a variety of shapes and styles. Once your puppy is past the chewing period you may want to consider getting a dog bed for him to sleep on. The dog bed could be used in the crate, and can also easily be taken out of the crate and brought to a different room in the house and placed on the floor as a place of his own to rest. When spending money on a dog bed for a young puppy, be aware that it may be soiled on or chewed, especially if the puppy is left alone for long periods of time.

Crib/Mattress Pads

These are flat rectangular pads that are made to be placed in a baby's crib under their crib sheet, to protect the mattress from overnight accidents.

They are very handy to use in the puppy's crate, over the top of the dog bed, or on the car seat. They are also handy to use when your dog is wet from swimming at the lake and needs to get in your car. They absorb liquid without letting it go through to the surface below.

Treats

Treats that are small are best for your puppy.

Plan on having some treats available in the house and for carrying with you. (By treats we mean any food item that can be used as a reward for a job well done.) There are many different manufacturers of dog treats. You've probably seen them in your supermarket and pet stores. Our suggestion when selecting store-bought dog treats is to choose something with as few chemicals as possible and, ideally, treats that are soft and can be broken into very small pieces. There are many web sites and online stores that offer a wide variety of healthy treats for dogs. You may also want to consider using cooked meat (chicken, steak, etc.) that you cut into small pieces, hot dogs, cheese, or vegetables. If your puppy likes it, it is a treat for him. Remember to make the pieces small, since any treat in great quantities will cause an upset stomach and loose stool.

"If dogs could talk, it would take a lot of the fun out of owning one."
—Andy Rooney

Section 2

Puppies Will Be Puppies

Chapter 4

The Importance of Socialization

Socialization is about having good experiences or having experiences without being fearful. We hope we can guide you in learning more about the importance of proper socialization and how it affects your life with both your puppy and children.

You must work on socializing your puppy in as many different places and situations as possible. Your puppy must get used to having people and other dogs coming onto your property (yard and house), so he will understand how to behave in those situations. Keep in mind that inviting other children over to play with the puppy has risks and benefits. Just as you will find children who will behave appropriately around dogs, there are some children who are afraid of dogs and might run and scream every time the puppy moves. There are also children who will interact in a very rough and physical manner with a puppy. Adult supervision is critical when socializing your puppy with children.

The Issue of Poor Socialization

For many years, we have been observing poorly socialized pups. Their behaviors and ability to learn are quite deficient. If a puppy is isolated from the world early on, he will have difficulty enjoying companionships. He may exhibit distrust or even extreme fear of any social contact and appear to have behavioral disabilities. These dogs typically appear to learn more slowly than the average dog and become easily frustrated when they are forced to problem solve, because fear or avoidance overrides all. We've had clients tell us they think their dog has ADD. Poorly socialized puppies appear to be unable to cope with life, and that is not the kind of dog you want if you have children. What parents want in a dog is one who can easily cope with the antics of children.

Socializing your young puppy with other dogs is critical.

According to Steven Lindsay, author of *Handbook of Applied Dog Behavior and Training,* research has shown us that in cases where poor socialization has occurred, some pups can regain some tranquility through concentrated remedial socialization. However, they may never reach the full potential they could have if things had been handled correctly from the onset.

Socialization Outside the Home

Socialization does not only occur at home. If your pup spends most of his time in your home and yard, with little exposure to the rest of the world, he may not fare well with strangers, other dogs, or new situations. You must develop good, long-lasting social skills, and you can accomplish this with daily walks and trips into public places for the life of your dog (not just the first year or two). When you and your pup are out and about, make sure your puppy is enjoying himself. If your pup becomes frightened when cars pass by, you may want to begin by walking him on a quiet street where there is less traffic and cars are traveling at slower speeds. Taking him to a busy downtown area may not be the best place for him until he becomes more comfortable with the movement and noise of cars. The key is that your pup enjoys every outing.

Socialization with Other Dogs

Socializing your young puppy with other dogs is critical. A 7-week-old puppy does not play the same as a 16-week-old puppy, nor will he play like a

2-year-old dog. When our children are young, we initially begin to socialize them with children of similar ages. You would not permit your 5-year-old son to go out on a Saturday night with his 18-year-old brother and friends! It's only after we recognize that our children can make decisions and speak up for themselves that we gradually expand upon their socialization with children of various ages. Be just as cautious when you are socializing your puppy to other dogs.

Socializing a puppy with a social, but unfamiliar dog is critically important to his development.

Keep in mind that a 2-year-old, unsocialized adult dog running loose in a dog park can easily injure and frighten your puppy. This experience could have an everlasting negative effect; therefore, we do *not* recommend dog parks for young puppies. As a dear friend and colleague, Trish King, said, "A dog park is like a cocktail party, where you don't know anyone and everyone is drunk. You could have fun, but it could be a disaster." If you see a puppy in a puppy class with a play style that is completely out of control, inevitably the owner will admit they've been socializing their puppy "at the local dog park." Unfortunately, these pups are learning to be disobedient, overly aroused by the sight of other dogs, and their play style is radically different from other pups who leave their litters and start their socialization in a safe, controlled environment.

Many people have multiple dogs in the home. It is important to understand that, just because a puppy is living with another dog, it doesn't mean the pup will grow up to be a social dog. We've found that most owners who have more than one dog do not spend the time to socialize their dogs with "non-family" dogs. They assume that since their dog gets along so well with the other resident dog, he will be fine with all dogs. This is a huge misconception, and trouble will result if you plan on taking your dog into public places or inviting new dogs over for a picnic or barbqueue. We are raised with siblings, yet our parents encourage us to make new friends. They do not expect that we can get along with others simply because we have a brother or sister.

Ongoing Socialization

With our own children, we send them off to school, believing that isolating them at home would not be beneficial for them. And, even though you begin the socialization process at a young age, you do not discourage your children from continuing on with their socialization once they are out of high school. You would be concerned if your child suddenly isolated himself to his room and didn't want to interact with friends. Why then are we not concerned about continuing our dog's socialization?

While socializing your puppy is critical, ongoing socialization, especially around children, is even more important. If the dog has not been exposed to children for several years, there is no guarantee that he will be comfortable around them in future years, or make a good pet for your child.

Socialization with Children

Socializing your puppy with children of all ages (infants, toddlers, elementary school), as well as different races and nationalities is critical. If, at any time, your puppy appears to be overwhelmed or frightened, you are probably moving too quickly, or the situation is not conducive for socialization. A child's birthday party or a greeting at the bus stop would *not* be the first choice for socializing your puppy to children, nor would the local State Fair. The level of noise and number of people may be too overwhelming for your puppy. You should start slow—try bringing the puppy to the bus stop when there are only one or two children present. Establish rules for the children and, if they cannot abide by

Socializing your puppy with children of all ages is critical.

them, they should not be permitted to pet your puppy. All greetings should be done in a calm fashion and not last for more than a few minutes at a time. You know you are on the right track if your puppy starts seeking children out.

Special Concerns When Socializing Small Dogs and Children

Unfortunately, some people treat small dogs like children, without realizing that they still go through the same

Socializing with a well-mannered child.

developmental stages as large dogs. It's so easy to coddle, cradle, and carry small dogs around. Children see this behavior, but they don't have the understanding that the small dog is not a furry stuffed toy who can easily get hurt if dropped, stepped on, or squeezed too tightly. If your decision is to get a small dog, your children will require extra supervision, since a small dog tends to sit on your lap or on the furniture, and ends up at a higher elevation than larger dogs. Children tend to hug, kiss, and squeeze dogs more often when they are off the floor and closer to the child's face level, which can lead to problems.

Poor Experiences with Handling

Imagine a puppy who was raised with children who constantly picked him up, hugged, and squeezed him, especially when he was trying to rest. This puppy certainly had a lot of experiences with children, but not pleasant ones. You will hopefully teach your children how to properly handle and interact with your puppy, but it is important to remember that your children's friends will not likely

Puppies are not stuffed animals. Too much handling, hugging, and squeezing can result in problems later on.

behave in the same manner. Also, keep in mind that too many children handling a puppy at one time can bring about fear in many pups. All interactions between puppies and children must be supervised for the well-being of all.

If you have children, think back to the time when you brought your baby home from the hospital. Everyone wanted to visit and hold the baby. Eventually, the infant began to cry, not enjoying being passed around like a doll and wanting the comfort of mother. No living creature enjoys this much handling, including your puppy.

Many people, without thinking, reach down and scoop puppies up, especially when they are sleeping. Puppies can learn to tolerate this, but being picked up and carried around is typically not something that puppies enjoy. They have four legs and like to spend their hours investigating on their own feet. Picture a 6-foot-tall gentleman walking over to a sleeping puppy and scooping him up simply because he is adorable. It's likely that being scooped up 6 feet in the air is not a pleasant feeling for the puppy. It's comparable to the feeling one might have on an amusement park ride where you are projected into the air—from 0 to 60 miles per hour in no time at all. Those puppies who find the constant picking up and holding to be unpleasant will hit a threshold later in life and may end up taking it out on the children. Enough is enough.

When To Stop Socialization?

The answer is never! Once again, compare your puppy's development with your child's. We are careful to start our children's education as early as possible. We tend to socialize with people who have children so that our children can learn good social skills. We do not limit our children's socialization to only their siblings.

A key factor when trying to determine if a particular experience is good for your puppy is to put yourself in your puppy's mind and body and ask yourself if you would tolerate what the puppy is going through. More important, would you enjoy it? Puppies should not have to *tolerate* children—they should *like* them.

Never stop socializing your puppy.

CASE STUDY

The Overwhelmed Puppy

A well-meaning puppy owner wanted to ensure that her puppy, Duke, grew up to be good with children and enjoy the world. She took daily trips out into public, exposing Duke to as many new things as possible. One day, she decided to take Duke to her son's soccer game, which could have been beneficial to the puppy. It was a good idea with good intentions; however, Duke did not have a good experience. As we know, children cannot resist touching, picking up, hugging, or holding a puppy. Duke was touched by "hundreds of children" she proudly told us. "How many children touched him at one time?" we asked. "I couldn't keep count" was her answer. Duke's owner thought she was doing the right thing by exposing him to as many children as possible, but because it happened all at the same time, the encounter was too overwhelming for Duke, and he began to back away when anyone approached him.

Put yourself in this puppy's place. You go to watch your nephew's soccer game and hundreds of children run over to you and start putting their hands all over your body; you would probably jump into your car and leave.

The Puppy Who Didn't Want to Be Held

Recently, a client was having a difficult time restraining and massaging her 12-week-old puppy, Cassie. When she attempted to cradle the puppy, the pup became very annoyed and exhibited what looked like a toddler having a temper tantrum. Cassie was in no way frightened, she simply did not want to be held. The client said the puppy was biting family members more often and with greater force. In order to help the owner, as well as to determine why Cassie was behaving in this manner, Pia sat on the floor and cradled her. The pup struggled to be released. Pia calmly told Cassie, "Stop it" and was happy to see that she settled down quite easily. When she began the massage, Cassie became quite relaxed and gave a sigh of relief. Pia then spoke to the mother and asked what was going on at home. The client said *she* had no problem with the massage, but *the children* were not succeeding. Bingo! There was the answer. There were three boys at home all under the age of ten. The parents had been told by a family member who recently started to train dogs that the children needed to be "dominant" over the puppy in order for the puppy to respect them. In order to achieve dominance, the owners were told to have the children roll the puppy over onto her back and hold her there until she was calm and avoided eye contact. They were told that if they didn't succeed with this exercise, Cassie would bite them one day. The poor pup had enough with these children, and being restrained by them turned into an unpleasant experience.

Their homework for the week was to have the children stop the exercise. The parents were to cradle and massage Cassie, while the boys could play with her, feed her, and give her treats for sitting and lying down when asked. Within a week, Cassie turned into a wet noodle in the arms of the mother when she was cradled. The owner was ready to give up on this puppy and almost returned her to the breeder, thinking Cassie was the wrong puppy for their household. Seeing her grin from ear to ear is part of why we enjoy our line of work as much as we do.

Always supervise while your child is handling the puppy.

Chapter 5

Puppy Behavior

Some puppy behaviors are normal, and some signify a potential problem. The following guidelines will help you determine whether or not your puppy is exhibiting normal puppy behavior. If you have concerns, take a proactive approach immediately by calling the puppy's breeder or the shelter/organization you adopted the puppy from and explain your concerns to them. Thereafter, you should seek out the assistance of a professional in the field to help you assess whether or not your concerns are justifiable.

Early Normal Puppy Behaviors

Mouthing

Your puppy is spending more time than you would like mouthing and biting at the children.

This could be because the kids are running, playing, screaming, or being silly. The sudden, rapid movements and loud noises of children excite most pups. Puppies don't understand that chasing after and catching moving, screaming children is unacceptable behavior. Many pups will remain excited even after the children stop. These are all signals to you that your puppy has probably not had enough exercise and is releasing all of his pent-up energy on the kids. If possible, take the entire family outside for some playtime.

Lack of Interest in the Children

Your puppy seems to be much more attached to and interested in you than the children.

Puppies enjoy being with leaders.

This will likely occur if the puppy spends the majority of his time with you, and you are the primary caretaker for the puppy—you feed, walk, and train him. All of this helps develop a close bond between you and the puppy, because the puppy is learning that you are in control, and you control all resources (food, fun, etc.). Puppies enjoy being with leaders. They play with their littermates, but snuggle with their mother when it's time to relax and feel safe. This behavior remains even after they have left their canine pack.

Not Listening

Your puppy doesn't listen to the children as diligently as you would like.

Children tend to get frustrated much more quickly than adults, especially when things are not going their way, or they are having a difficult time getting through to the puppy. If a puppy doesn't understand what the child is asking, most pups will go off and do something else. Instead of letting him go or asking for help, your child might chase the pup down, grab hold of his tail to stop him from leaving, and repeat the commands over and over again. Look at it from the puppy's perspective—this nagging, annoying behavior is not very enjoyable, nor is the interaction.

Housetraining Issues

Your puppy seems to be taking a long time to housetrain.

Don't get frustrated. Housetraining can take several months, depending on the puppy and your diligence. Make sure that you or another adult are taking on the primary responsibility for this training process. If you put this responsibility on the children, it's not fair to them or the puppy. Children will likely forget to take the pup out and, when they do take him out, they may not pay attention to whether or not the puppy actually relieved himself.

If you have any concerns about a behavior that your puppy is exhibiting, please see a professional.

Playing with Toys
The puppy is constantly picking up the children's toys instead of his own toys.

Puppies cannot distinguish between their stuffed toys and your child's toys lying right next to each other on the family-room carpet. What's on the floor is up for grabs (at least at this age).

Fear of Dog Parks
When you take your puppy to the local dog park, he appears frightened.

We do not recommend dog parks for young puppies. Puppies like to investigate their surroundings and interact with other dogs at their own pace. A puppy going into a dog park might be rushed by ten dogs who want to check him out all at once. This is not a pleasant experience for most puppies. He may become severely frightened and even injured.

Early Puppy Behaviors You Should Be Concerned About
The following behaviors may not be serious problems, depending on the nature of the behavior, the situation, and the events surrounding the occurrence. However, if they are not dealt with early on, they could develop into serious problems later in life. They all warrant your immediate attention. If you ever have any concerns about a behavior that your puppy

is exhibiting, please see a professional in the field. Behaviors typically do not simply "go away with age"—they usually get worse!

Fearful of New Situations

You have taken every precautionary measure to properly socialize your puppy, yet the puppy appears to be anxious, timid, or frightened in most new situations.

You are afraid that your puppy is not becoming properly socialized, and his behavior seems to be getting worse. Continuing to socialize the puppy in your current manner may do more harm than good. Your puppy may be overwhelmed with the type of exposure, the amount of exposure, or the environment in which it is occurring. Scale back on the amount of socialization and call a professional for an evaluation. Puppies should be curious about things, not exhibit extreme fear; puppies should enjoy investigating, not become traumatized and crawl into your lap. Puppies might be cautious, but they typically bounce back well.

Hiding

Your puppy seems to spend a lot of time hiding under furniture or in his crate.

When you or your child reach for the puppy or take him from his safe haven, the puppy curls his lips, shows his teeth, growls, snarls, or snaps at you or your children. There may be several reasons for this behavior. Many people think they must have startled the puppy or the puppy did not hear them and that is why he reacted. While this may occur on occasion, it should not occur each and every time. Also, you may be disturbing the puppy too often during his down time and have inadvertently put him on alert. Puppies require downtime, especially if you are giving them adequate exercise. Establish a rule with your children that they are *not* permitted to bother the puppy when he is sleeping. If things seem to get better, then stay on track. If the puppy's behavior becomes worse, or if you can truly say that you have not been bothering him, then you should be concerned.

Toy Guarding

When you give your puppy a new bone or toy, he immediately takes it to his favorite hiding spot or crate.

If you or your child attempt to take the object from your puppy's mouth, your puppy growls, snarls, curls his lip, snaps, or bites. This is a serious problem, especially at such a young age. Please refer to Chapter 12 for tips on how to avoid resource guarding.

Ignoring Cues

Your puppy rarely responds to his name or other cues.

Guarding toys can become a serious problem.

While this may not be dangerous, there is legitimate concern, since most puppies enjoy training, especially when you use rewards in your training. Usually, puppies are like little sponges, and the more you teach them, the more they want to learn. If you feel behaviors have been properly taught and the puppy still does not respond, we recommend reevaluating what type of methodology you are using. When you set a puppy up to succeed by helping him understand what you want, and then reward him for his compliance, the puppy should be happy to respond. If you feel that you are constantly punishing him or become upset when he isn't listening, you may be frightening the puppy or teaching him to ignore you, since he doesn't understand what is expected. He is probably not responding because he doesn't know how.

Resistance To Grooming

Whenever you attempt to groom your puppy, he goes ballistic.

Is he simply fooling around and being bratty, or is his behavior over the top? Most puppies will mouth or bite at the grooming instruments and your hands, but he should not turn into a little piranha ready for his next meal just because he sees the brush.

Afraid of the Veterinarian or Groomer

Puppies should be curious, silly, and playful.

When you take your puppy to your veterinarian or groomer, they have to pin him down or muzzle him in order to examine him, or give him a vaccine or bath.

It is possible that his behavior is due to the events that happen at the veterinarian or groomer (painful shots or pain during grooming), but not necessarily. If the pup has been frightened or had painful experiences, he will most likely shake and quiver. It is recommended that you make as many trips to your veterinarian's office as possible during the early months for no reason other than to give him treats and have fun. If your puppy's only association with the veterinarian is to get stuck with a needle, then he may not like going for visits. This may not be a concern for you now, but once he is 80 pounds, it will be more difficult for you and more stressful for your dog. If your puppy behaves in this manner whenever any stranger tries to handle him, this is the sign of a serious problem.

Food Guarding

When you put your puppy's food bowl down, he gulps his food very fast, as if he is anxious about someone taking it away.

Or, he may do the opposite and stop eating whenever you or your children walk near him. He may growl, snarl, snap, or bite when you attempt to touch him while eating or take his bowl away. If worked on early, you should be able to get your puppy to feel more comfortable around his bowl when he is eating. Until you can speak to an expert, do not have your children feed him. Taking your puppy's food bowl away to prove that you can is fine as long as it is not done often and so long as the puppy is not exhibiting aggression. If you decide to take his food bowl away, we always recommend putting something yummy into the bowl when you put it back. This way, the puppy learns that when the bowl is removed, something better than

Your puppy should feel comfortable around his food bowl when he is eating.

his kibble is returned to him. See Chapter 12 for more on food bowl problems.

Disinterest in People and Dogs

Your puppy has no interest in people, dogs, or even both, and tends to avoid them.

This is a concern, and you should seek professional assistance since puppies should be curious, silly, and playful.

Growling and Snarling

The pup has curled his lip, growled, snarled, or snapped at other dogs, children, or adults.

Take note of when the behavior occurs and in what context. Again, this is quite serious behavior in a young puppy and will not likely go away without intervention.

Just Tolerating Children
The puppy appears to tolerate children.

The word "tolerate" is unacceptable when it comes to dogs and children. Dogs must *like* children, not simply *tolerate* them. Be familiar with some of the more subtle warning signs from your puppy's body language when he is becoming uncomfortable around children. If you see any of these signs, you should immediately intervene to avoid a bite incident. Some body language to watch for in your puppy when your child (or anyone, for that matter) is interacting with him are as follows: yawning and licking his lips or nose; scratching himself or continued shaking (as if he were wet); grooming himself; licking paws; sniffing the ground; rapid panting; raised tail (over the back); fur on neck or back standing up (also known as hackles); ears laid back; whale eye (looking from the corner of the eye so you see the whites of his eye). All of these behaviors are a signal to you that the pup is not comfortable. Even if your puppy seems to enjoy being handled roughly by kids, it is important to know when enough is enough.

Even issues that are really "normal" canine behavior still need to be dealt with. Aggression is a "normal" behavior in dogs, yet it is unacceptable in the human world. Chapter 8 has more on canine body language, and the Resources section has our list of recommended reading and references to further help educate you in canine body language and behaviors.

Needs vs. Wants

We all have needs and wants, and so does your puppy. If you give your puppy everything he wants too often, you will probably end up with a very spoiled dog who constantly demands your attention. On the other hand, when a puppy doesn't get what he wants, he may, out of frustration, exhibit inappropriate behaviors, such as barking, jumping, biting, and otherwise annoying the family members.

You Decide When Playtime Ends

Let's assume that your puppy loves to play with a tennis ball. You have taken care of feeding and exercising your puppy, perhaps by taking him out and throwing the ball for him, and now you would like to sit on the sofa and read a book. While reading, your puppy brings his tennis ball over and drops it in your lap—he still wants to play. You ignore him, so he picks up the ball again and tosses it toward you and nudges you with his nose. You decide to throw the ball for him to keep him happy and get him to stop bothering you so you can read your book. The puppy goes and gets the ball and brings it back and repeats the process of dropping it in your lap. The more you cater to his wants, the more persistent he will be in demanding that you comply with his request. After you've thrown the ball eight times while trying to read, you decide that you have had enough and you refuse to throw it. Your puppy will now resort to even more annoying behaviors, like barking at you, pawing at you, or tugging your pants leg in order to get you to throw the ball. After all, *he* wasn't done playing.

Your responsibility as a new puppy owner is to ensure that the puppy's *needs* are being met. What are a puppy's needs? They are food and water, a warm, dry place to sleep, and sufficient exercise, including both physical and mental stimulation. Puppies who are not getting enough food, exercise, and uninterrupted rest may become cranky, resulting in excessive mouthing, hyperactivity, or vocalization. Almost everyone knows that a puppy needs food, water, and a place to sleep, but the need to provide sufficient exercise and mental stimulation are often overlooked by most dog owners. Meeting his exercise needs will help you to have a more content, calm puppy who will learn to rest when in the house. A tired puppy is a good puppy! However, it's important to meet his exercise needs without catering to his wants. Take your puppy out to play or for a walk before he tells you that he wants to play.

He may still want to play when you come back into the house, but simply show him that you are done by ignoring his demands. Do not give in to his cute look and silly antics. If you have given him enough time and exercise, he will eventually stop trying and lie down to rest.

Puppies need to learn to accept the adults in the household as their leaders.

Drs. Suzanne Hetts and Daniel Estep, applied animal behaviorists from Colorado, were instrumental in discussing and writing about needs vs. wants in dogs many years ago. See the recommended reading list in the Resources section for more information.

Learning

To live in harmony with their human families, puppies need to learn to accept the adults in the household as their leaders and the children as their best friends. We discourage trying to make your children be the puppy's leader. Simply put, many of us are in the work force, but not all of us are in an upper management position. Most of us report to a superior and, in order for us to respect and trust our superiors, they must exhibit fairness, confidence, emotional control, and consistency. They should keep us safe and attempt to build a rapport with us since we are part of their team. Your puppy needs the same qualities from his leader. Children certainly don't need this added burden put upon them, nor are the majority of them capable of handling the task. It requires training for a puppy to learn to accept adults as his leaders and to learn good manners. A trained dog walks nicely on lead, comes when called, and accepts restraint and handling by you, family members, your veterinarian, and groomer. He chews on appropriate objects and relieves himself outdoors. Puppies must also learn to tolerate being left alone, stop barking when told and, most important, never place their teeth on people. All of these things must be taught to your puppy by you, his leader, and we firmly believe it cannot and should not be a task left up to your children.

"He Knows He Is Wrong"

Teaching your puppy to learn the rules of your house can take 1 to 2 years, depending upon the size, breed, and maturity of your puppy. It is important to remember that puppies know absolutely nothing about right from wrong. To say, "He knows he was wrong" is beyond the mental capability of the puppy. What puppies do know and understand is "safe" versus "dangerous." Their behaviors are always under the control of consequences—it is either safe or dangerous to do something, rewarding or not rewarding—not right or wrong, as we think. If a particular behavior brought about something good for the puppy, and it was safe to do, the behavior will continue. If the behavior brought about something unpleasant to the puppy and it felt dangerous, the behavior will cease. For example, why don't most dogs try to steal a juicy steak sizzling on a nice hot grill? The aroma of the meat is most powerful during the cooking stage; yet they wait for the food to be removed from those hot areas and placed on a platter before attempting to steal it. Leave the steak on the grill until it completely cools down and you can be assured that the pup will try to grab it, since the "punishment" (getting burned by the grill) is gone. It is now safe to try to steal the food.

An example of another activity that puppies learn is safe and rewarding is taking things from the laundry or wastebasket. What could be so exciting about a dirty sock or a tissue? Perhaps puppies just like to chew on them, or they like that the whole family gets excited and chases them once they have the items. This activity is rewarding to the puppy and safe to do in the act. If you'd like to try to discourage this behavior, try putting a highly bitter tasting deterrent in your wastebasket. You can bet your pup will pull his nose out quickly and look for something else to do, once he figures out it's not quite as rewarding as he thought.

Learning Takes Time

Be aware that the pup will take some time to learn your household rules. The rate at which your puppy will learn will depend on the puppy and how much time and effort you put into the training process. During this learning

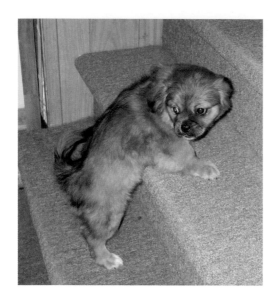

Get your puppy acclimated to stairs at an early age.

process, you can bet that he will make some mistakes. Are you going to be tolerant of these mistakes, or will you quickly give up and loose your cool? Will you forgive your puppy and instead get angry with yourself for not adequately watching him, or will you take it out on the pup? Are you ready for the pup to have an accident on your carpet? Will you be able to stay on top of your pup so he doesn't chew your new sofa? You must have patience when training a puppy or dog and be prepared for the mistakes he will make. Learn to forgive and forget. Puppies do not hold grudges—make sure that you do not either!

Getting Over Fears

Most puppies will end up in a situation at some point early in their lives that frightens or worries them. They may require encouragement, help, and support from you in order to get over the experience. For example, if the puppy is exhibiting fear about going up or down a staircase, you should help him learn how to go up and down without concern. To go up the stairs, start off by placing the puppy on the top step and allow him to go up one step. Take one step at a time. For most puppies, it is less frightening to go up than down. To help him learn how to go down, start on the bottom step and allow him to go down one step. Never get annoyed, frustrated, or angry at your puppy if he is frightened or worried about performing a certain activity (like step climbing). This will only make it worse.

Stealing and the Game of Chase

Time after time, you scold your puppy for taking your sneaker, but the next chance he gets, he steals it again! You wonder what is wrong with him. You let him know that you do not like this behavior, yet he continues to do it anyway. Puppies stealing items that are not theirs is a very common problem. They steal all sorts of objects like shoes, laundry, tissues, and the kid's toys. There are several reasons why they might steal, but you can prevent them from happening.

The Thrill of the Chase

One of the most fun and exciting games a puppy likes to play is chase. Puppies especially love to chase the kids as they are running, screaming, and waving their arms in the air. Some puppies love to be chased. Even though they love it, chase games should be discouraged since they usually don't end in a positive way. Keep in mind that a good chase does not always start out intentionally as a chase. It usually develops as a result of something the puppy has done, like steal your sneaker. The puppy picks the sneaker up in his mouth, and someone in the family spots him and yells, "He has the sneaker!" Everyone gets up in a flurry of excitement and commotion and heads toward the puppy. The puppy's ears go up and his eyes open wide as he runs the other way with your sneaker while everyone chases after him. The puppy thinks, "What fun, we should do this every day!" It doesn't matter that, when you finally catch him, you take the sneaker back and scold him for what he did. The thrill of the chase was wonderful; the reprimand wasn't that bad. He is learning what to do in order to get the whole family in an uproar and start the great game of chase: seek out and steal that sneaker.

Preventing the Chase Game

The more success your puppy has at stealing items and starting chase games, the more difficult it will be to get rid of the behavior. So, how can you prevent this from becoming a big time-consuming headache and behavior problem for you?

The first and easiest thing to do is to keep those items that the puppy likes to steal out of reach. Your sneakers should go in the closet, and the closet door must be closed. If stealing from the wastebasket is a problem, close the door or put the wastebasket under the sink or behind a cabinet door. If the puppy is stealing clothes from the laundry basket, put it on top of the washing machine. If stealing the kid's toys is a fun pastime, then get your children to put their toys away when they are done with them (imagine how neat and tidy your house will be as a result). Once your puppy destroys a valued toy, the children learn very quickly that they need to pay close attention to your instructions.

KEEP IN MIND

The Toy Room

It's not easy to get children to put their toys away. Having a new puppy in the house who will experiment by chewing and stealing everything he can find will cause you to have to make some adjustments. We recommend, if possible, that one room in the house be designated as a toy room/play area, where the toys live and are allowed on the floor in that room only. (If you don't have a room to use as a toy room, then use your child's bedroom.) The door to that room should be kept closed. To interrupt any theft attempts, the puppy should only be allowed in that room when you are with him.

The second thing you can do to help prevent the puppy from stealing is to set up the house rule: *do not chase the puppy if he has stolen something*. This is the hardest thing for most people to do. Rules and reason go out the window when you see your puppy with your new dress shoes that you need to wear tonight. Panic sets in over the thought of the damage that might be done to the stolen item, and the chase begins. "Ah ha! Success!" thinks the puppy. Following the "do not chase the puppy" rule is hard enough for adults; it is even more difficult for young children. Young children love to run and are easily excited—just like your puppy.

Don't Allow Chasing

Most children typically shriek, "No!" as soon as the puppy gets their toy in his mouth. The excitement in their voice and the arms flailing in the air may cause the puppy to prick up his ears and get ready to bolt. "No!" becomes a signal to the pup that if he gets up and runs with the item, a chase begins. What follows usually is a child shouting, "No! No! No!" and running as fast as possible through the house with arms waving, chasing the puppy, while the puppy has the time of his life running from him or her. Why wouldn't he keep taking the toys? What fun for him! Needless to say, this behavior by both child and puppy must be stopped immediately. That way, once the puppy matures, the child's toys can probably be left on the floor, and the puppy will not likely take them.

The third and slightly more advanced thing that you can do to prevent the puppy from stealing or putting something in his mouth is to teach the "leave it" cue. The puppy learns that "leave it" means "do not put your mouth on that object." We highly encourage you to take your puppy to obedience training classes and seek out the assistance of a dog trainer to help you teach "leave it" to your puppy!

Retrieving the Stolen Item

If your puppy does steal something, you will need to get it back. Do your best to remain calm while you walk up to the puppy. He will eventually stop moving if you are calm. If you have taught him to relinquish an object on cue (outlined in Chapter 10), you can try that. If he relinquishes the object, praise him and get him something else to play with. If he will not let go, hold on to his collar and calmly sit there with him until he drops the item. Most puppies will not hold it for long.

You can also try walking away from him and doing one of the following: go to the kitchen and make noises like you are preparing his meal or opening the

Make sure your puppy receives the proper amount of exercise.

cookie jar; or prepare to go outside by getting your shoes and coat on and heading toward the door. He may come running as a result of these actions and chances are that he has dropped the stolen item somewhere along the way. Ask him to sit when he gets to you and reward him for complying. You are not rewarding the stealing, you are rewarding the last behavior the dog performed—in this case, the sit.

If he happens to still have the stolen item in his mouth when he gets to you, he will need to drop it to receive his reward. He gets the reward, you get the shoe. In this case, you are rewarding the puppy for giving up the object. There are some smart pups who will pick up the sneaker and bring it to you in hopes of getting that treat—not to worry. Once the pup is performing this behavior, petting and praising him will be enough of a reward. Once he drops the item, you can then redirect him to one of his toys.

Be careful not to bribe the puppy to retrieve the stolen item. A bribe might look like this: You have said, "Give" and your puppy looks at you with the object in his mouth and runs the other way. You avoid the chase game and instead go to the cookie jar, get a treat out, show it to him, and say, "Give." You have now successfully bribed him into giving up the object. If you always do this, your pup will quickly learn never to give up the object until you go for a treat. This is certainly not what you want. After the puppy has learned "Give," the treat can be used as a reward to reinforce the proper behavior. You may have to bribe if the situation is dangerous to your puppy (such as something sharp or poisonous in his mouth), but *only* if the situation is dangerous.

Stealing for Attention

Another reason why your puppy might be stealing items is to get attention. You have undoubtedly heard of children purposely doing things that they've been told not to, simply because they learn that it will cause their parents to pay attention to them. Even though it is not a happy, enjoyable type of attention or interaction, in the child's mind it is better than no interaction at all. A puppy who is not receiving the proper amount of exercise, mental stimulation, and human interaction may do the same thing. He knows grabbing the sock out of the hamper will get everyone excited and interacting with him. To avoid this, make sure you are giving your puppy enough attention.

Be careful not to bribe the puppy to retrieve the stolen item.

Your puppy needs to be physically exercised and mentally stimulated, and will greatly enjoy interacting with you through play, petting, and learning new obedience exercises. Remember, a tired puppy is a good puppy. If he is tired from receiving sufficient exercise, training, and human interaction, then he will be content to rest quietly on the floor as the family goes about their business.

Chapter 6

Puppy Training

Obedience training is important for all dogs, but even more so if children will be in the home. We highly recommend taking your dog to a qualified dog trainer who will teach you how to train your dog. Never think that your dog is too old or that it is too late to start the training process. Obviously, it will be easier if you begin training your dog when he is just a puppy, but an adult dog can still be trained. You *can* teach an old dog new tricks. A little practice every day will go a long way toward making your dog a more well-mannered member of the household and help alleviate any concern that you might have about his interactions with children. Listed below are just a few basic, yet important exercises to start teaching your puppy or dog.

Obedience Training for Good Manners

Teach the Puppy His Name

One of your first training responsibilities is to teach your puppy his name. We understand what names mean and that they identify a particular person, but your puppy does not. He does not understand this concept, nor does he understand human language. His name is just another sound to him—he must learn that you expect a particular behavior from him when you say it. That behavior, at a minimum, is to have your puppy *look at you* (make eye contact) when you say his name. To start, whenever your puppy looks into your eyes, tell him "Yes!" and reward him with something that he likes. This could be a treat, his favorite toy, petting, or trip outdoors for some playtime. Once he begins to associate looking at you with a reward, he will probably make eye contact with you more often. As soon as he is about to look into your eyes, say his name. The sound of his name will now be paired with the desired behavior: *look at me*. Always make it rewarding for him to respond to his name by making eye contact with you. You should use a pleasant tone of voice during this training, and always reward your puppy for giving the desired response. Never say your puppy's name in a harsh tone or follow it with something unpleasant to him. For example, if you say his name and he comes to you and, instead of a reward, you immediately cut his nails, he will find this experience unpleasant, and begin to associate bad things with his name. Or perhaps you continually use your puppy's name in conjunction with punishment. Chances are he will stop looking at you and instead run away when he hears his name. The same theory holds true for teaching other behaviors.

No Jumping

Many people encourage their dogs to jump up on them. While this is your own personal choice to make, it is important to remember that if you allow your dog to jump on you, he will also think it is perfectly acceptable to jump on other people. A jumping dog is likely to knock down and frighten small children. You should also keep in mind that if you are planning to start a family, there will be an expectant mother in the house. You will not want your dog jumping up on a pregnant woman's stomach several times a day. You will also need to be careful when carrying an infant in your arms. If your dog is large or has a

Keeping things as simple as possible for your dog will make it much easier for him.

high reach when he jumps, he may land on the infant as he brings his feet down to rest on you. An infant could easily be injured by the dog's toenails or his body weight. It is not easy for the dog to understand why you are yelling at him for jumping up on you when you have a baby in your arms, if he is typically allowed to do so any other time. Keeping things as simple as possible for the dog will make it much easier for him. If you currently allow your dog to jump up on you, we recommend that you stop encouraging that behavior.

Many people inadvertently give the dog attention when he jumps on them. After they calmly and gently

This puppy's over-exuberant greeting behavior could result in the child being knocked down.

push him off, once his paws are on the floor they pet him. They do not realize that this only encourages the jumping behavior. One rule to help get rid of or prevent a jumping problem is to never touch the dog if he jumps up—not even to push him off. Show him that he will get no attention from you if he performs this behavior. Fold your arms and turn you back on him if necessary. Only pet and touch him when all four of his feet are on the ground.

Taking Treats Gently

How does your puppy react when you give him a treat? How does he take it from your hand when you offer it to him? Does he gently take it or do you feel his teeth on your fingers? If your puppy gets excited when you offer him a goody and quickly grabs at it, not caring about your hand getting in the way, think about how this will feel to a young child or baby. The pain of the puppy's teeth on the child's hand is one problem. The child could also become afraid

Teeth should not be used when taking treats from your hand.

of dogs because of this interaction. You must teach your puppy to take treats gently from hands and to do so only when given permission.

Teaching the puppy to take treats by permission only is especially important if there will be little children around. The hands of a small child are at a perfect height to grab food out of for at most any size dog or puppy. It happens all the time. Children often hold food in such a way that it looks like they are offering it to the dog, even though they are not. You give your child a snack, and he happily takes this snack and walks around eating it, with the puppy eagerly following behind. At first opportunity, the puppy takes the snack from the child's hand, and it's gone. Now you have a crying child, or worse, a child who is now angry at the puppy and screams and whacks him for taking the snack. Stealing food from a child's hand is certainly bad manners and an unwanted behavior. The puppy must be taught that he may only take something from a person's hand when told. Here's how:

- First, you have to teach him to take the treat gently. Hold a treat in your fist and put your hand low in front of your puppy's nose. Open your fist, holding the treat with your fingers and let your puppy smell the treat. If you feel his teeth on your hand or fingers, in a deep stern voice say, "Ouch!" and close the treat in your fist. Repeat this process until the puppy no longer uses his teeth to grab at your hand, fingers, or the treat.
- Now that the puppy is using his tongue or lips to lick or pull the treat into his mouth (anything but his teeth), say, "Gentle" as he takes it. If, at any time, you feel the pup's teeth on your skin, you should not

allow the puppy to take the treat. Close your fist and take it away. Then try again.

- Once the puppy is taking treats gently, teach him to take food only when given permission. Hold a treat in your open palm, with your arm extended down by your side. If the puppy attempts to take the treat, close your fist. When the puppy eventually backs away from your fist, open it again. Repeat until the puppy no longer tries to take the treat. Then tell him, "Take it" and extend the treat toward him. Make sure he takes it gently! Practice several times per day until your puppy no longer reaches out to take something from your hand and instead waits for permission.

Children Offering Dogs Treats

Most children love to feed animals. It is very exciting to them. Most dog owners cannot take out a treat to give to their dogs without the children wanting to give them one as well. At least, they think they want to give the treat until they see the dog's mouth and teeth coming toward them to receive it. The sight of the oncoming teeth will usually make a child retract his hand, causing the dog to move toward the hand more quickly in order to get the treat that is now leaving. The dog may even bite at the hand as it moves away, to try to get the treat. A child might also move his or her hand straight up in the air away from the dog, causing the dog to jump up on them to reach it, possibly hurting the child with his toenails or knocking them over. Other children might become leery and toss the treat to the dog. The dog might leap forward in an attempt to catch the treat before it hits the ground, which can be intimidating to the child.

We suggest that you allow your young children to give treats only to dogs with good manners, who will gently take a treat and not grab the child's hand. For those dogs who you know are well mannered, teach your child to open his or her hand so it is a flat palm. Then, put the treat in the palm of the child's hand, rather than having him or her hold it with their fingers. Let the dog take the treat off the open palm.

Selecting a Qualified Dog Trainer

Dr. Ian Dunbar was instrumental in developing and encouraging people to take their puppies to a qualified trainer during the critical socialization period to get the pups off to the right start.

Seek out the assistance of a dog trainer who uses positive, reward-based training techniques.

We always recommend that new dog owners seek out the assistance of a dog trainer who uses positive, reward-based training techniques. Prior to enrolling, ask the trainer if you may drop in and observe a class. If the trainer will not permit you to watch (free of charge), we recommend that you look elsewhere. Avoid trainers who offer a guarantee that your puppy will be fully trained after a short 6 to 8 weeks. No one can guarantee a dog's behavior or the outcome of training. Since this is a critical time in your puppy's life, the trainer should have advanced knowledge in canine social behavior. Matching your puppy up with the right playmate and handling your puppy according to his temperament is instrumental in your puppy's success and future well-being.

For a list of trainers in your area, please visit the web site of the Association of Pet Dog Trainers at www.apdt.com. To find a certified pet dog trainer, visit the site of the Certification Council for Pet Dog Trainers at www.ccpdt.com.

Puppy Training Classes

We highly recommend taking your puppy to a puppy training class as early as possible. The class should include playtime with other puppies. You may notice that your puppy does not seem to be enjoying his socialization time with his classmates. He hides, runs away, glues himself to your legs, quivers, and wants to leave. Not all puppy classes are right for every puppy. The mix of puppies in the class is critical to the success of some, and will not matter at all to others. Your puppy should have fun in class, and should be pulling you into the classroom in anticipation of that fun. He should not be clinging to your side, or spending the entire time trying to leave. If he is, be sure to express your concerns to your instructor. Stress and anxiety interfere with new learning. If the environment overwhelms the puppy, the pup may shut down. If the pup is enjoying class, and the instructor has set the class up for success, he will try harder. He will develop good coping skills, as opposed to the "I can't, I won't" behavior exhibited by fearful pups. If the instructor does not exhibit compassion for your concerns and tells you the puppy is fine and will "get over it," go with your gut feeling and consider finding another puppy class.

During class, if your puppy comes running to you for help while being chased down during playtime by a 40-pound puppy ready to pounce on

Don't be afraid to scoop your puppy up if he comes running to you for help during puppy class.

him, by all means, scoop your puppy up. You are not reinforcing fear in your puppy, as you may have been told. You are saving him from a potentially bad experience that can have an everlasting effect on him.

Chapter 7

Housetraining and the Crate

Having a dog who is reliably housetrained is probably one of the main desires for all puppy owners. Constant management and supervision, in addition to knowing when and how often your puppy needs to eliminate, will help you to achieve this important goal. It is very important to set your puppy up for success by establishing a routine and being consistent. Housetraining is one of the biggest sources of frustration for most puppy owners. It takes a little extra time and a lot of patience on your part to get the puppy out at various times, in all kinds of weather, before he has an accident in the house. The time and effort that you invest now in your puppy's training process will pay off in the future!

Housetraining Your Puppy

Develop a Routine

Young puppies will do best with an established routine and schedule. Each puppy is an individual, but there are certain times most puppies will need to go out, for instance when children are around (since they tend to get puppies excited, causing them to need to relieve themselves). The following is a typical daily routine to help you gauge when your puppy may need to go out. It will help you stay on top of the situation before he has an opportunity to relieve himself indoors.

1. **As soon as he wakes up in the morning.**

2. **Fifteen minutes after the first trip out in the morning.**
   The puppy has probably picked up a toy, started chewing on a bone, played with the children, etc.; he'll need to go out after this time.

3. **Within 30 minutes after eating breakfast, lunch, and dinner.**
   You will need to judge the exact time based on the individual needs of your puppy. The half hour is a general guideline—it may be within 15 or 20 minutes for your puppy.

4. **Every 2 to 4 hours during the day, depending upon his activity level.**
   You must be prepared to make the commitment to get him out at least that often. There is no right or wrong schedule or specific amount of time that a puppy should be able to hold it—it will vary from puppy to puppy. You will need to determine the needs of your puppy and figure out when he needs to go.

5. **After excitement and play.**
   This is often the time that catches most puppy owners off guard. For example, you take the puppy outside; he urinates and defecates, so you bring him back in and allow him some house freedom, thinking it is safe for a while. The puppy proceeds to run around and play with the kids for 15 minutes, then suddenly stops and urinates on the floor. The excitement and running can cause him to need to eliminate. If he has been busy and active in the house for a number of minutes, and you notice that he has suddenly stopped the activity, quickly get him outside.

6. **After naps.**

7. **After chewing on bones.**

8. **Before going to bed.**
   Depending upon his age, the last trip out may be between 10:00 and 11:00 p.m. Once the puppy gets older, the last trip out might be 9:30 p.m.

9. **In the middle of the night.**

Typically, young pups will need to go out in the middle of the night for the first month. You may get lucky and have a puppy who can hold it for 5 or 6 hours during the night; but be prepared to get up early in the morning or possibly once during the night as well. You might want to set your alarm for a time just before your puppy usually gets up. That way, you can get up and take him out before he starts whining or barking to be let out. Eventually, when he does wake up in the middle of the night, you can begin to wait a bit longer before taking him out, teaching him to hold it. (Unless of course the pup seems to be extremely frantic. In that case, it is likely that he really needs to go—now!)

As the weeks go by, you may see that he sleeps throughout the night but wakes up early, say around 6:00 a.m. As he matures, he should be able to sleep a bit longer.

Out and In

When housetraining starts, immediately begin teaching your puppy "out" and "in." As you are taking the puppy outside, say, "Out." Wait for the puppy to relieve himself in your presence and praise him for this behavior. Then, quickly turn and run toward the door and say, "In." We like to reward our pups for coming in so it's just as enjoyable as going out. When you come in, head for the cookie jar and give him a treat. If you do this several times, you are patterning a chain of behaviors. The puppy learns to go out when you say, "Out," relieve

Establish a housetraining routine for your puppy, and always supervise when you bring him outside.

himself in your presence, and then quickly turn for the door when you say, "In."

Feed on a Schedule

If you feed your puppy on a regular schedule, it will be easier for you to know when he will need to eliminate. Avoid putting the puppy's food down on the floor and leaving it there indefinitely. Give him 20 minutes after you've put food in the bowl and, if he does not finish eating and has walked away, pick the bowl up and feed him the remainder at the next meal. If you allow him to snack on treats and other goodies, or pick at his food all day long, he will probably not eat his regular meals. If your children had a choice of cookies and ice cream, or chicken and veggies, which do you think they would choose? Monitoring what and when your puppy eats will greatly help you in the housetraining process. Once your puppy is housetrained, there is no need to stick to such a firm schedule.

Freedom To Roam the House?

As your puppy becomes more reliable, has fewer accidents in the house (perhaps once a week), and is eliminating outdoors most of the time, you can gradually start to give him more freedom in the house. At this stage "freedom" means moving about the rooms of the house *with you*, not on his own. Puppies still require supervision for many

Feed your puppy on a regular schedule.

reasons (like chewing inappropriate items). It is important that you are managing and supervising the puppy's activities while in the house, meaning that if he is not in his crate, he is close by you. By doing so, you will hopefully see the signs that he needs to go. For example, after he has been very busy, maybe even running around, he has now stopped and is sniffing the floor, walking in circles, heading toward a door, appearing antsy, etc. If you've been keeping an eye on him, you can quickly get him outside before he goes in the house. If too much freedom has given him the opportunity to have

Sending your puppy out alone to relieve himself will prolong the time it will take to successfully housetrain.

frequent accidents in the house, he may develop preferences for certain surfaces and indoor locations. Puppies quickly learn about surface preferences, and you don't want the carpet to be his first choice. Remember, puppies are not born understanding that urinating on the carpet is unacceptable. If he's successful going on these surfaces, it will make it that much harder to stop.

If you started to give your pup more space to wander, and he begins having accidents in the house, then go back to keeping him closer to you, and be sure he is in the same room with you at all times.

Never Send Your Puppy Out Alone

It is your job to teach your puppy that you want him to eliminate outdoors. In order to achieve this, you must always go outside with your puppy, even if you have a fenced yard. If he is outside alone, no one is there telling him that eliminating outdoors is the correct behavior. When you are present, you can praise him as he is relieving himself; you can also start to associate the behavior with a cue word by saying, "Hurry up" or "Do your business," etc. Once he comes back into the house, it is too late to reward him. To make your puppy understand that eliminating outside is the preferred behavior, you must be out there with him *each and every time.*

If your puppy is outside alone, you will also not know exactly when or where he is urinating or defecating. It is very important to know when a young puppy eliminates, because it will give you an idea as to when he might need to go again. It is also important to examine his feces for foreign objects or parasites. This will help to determine if he has eaten anything inappropriate, or perhaps if he is ill.

If you want your puppy to relieve himself in a certain area, then you may want to put him on a lead. Keep in mind that, if not supervised, male dogs may start lifting their legs to urinate on items in the yard, such as your lawn furniture, plants, even the side of the house or deck. You must be there to stop it from happening. If you don't care where he relieves himself outdoors, then there is no need for a leash as long as you have a fenced yard.

Puppies need to learn to relieve themselves whether on or off leash, in the backyard or on a walk, at the park or outside the veterinarian's office. A fun routine for the whole family is to take daily family walks together. Not only will this help to give your puppy some exercise and teach him to walk on leash, but he will also learn to eliminate in areas away from your yard, and it will help to involve the entire family in the housetraining process.

Get Help During the Day

If your regular schedule requires that your puppy will be left for long periods of time alone in his crate, then we recommend having a pet sitter, friend, or neighbor come in to take your puppy out for exercise and to eliminate outdoors. It is not fair to the puppy to give him no option other than to go in his crate because he has been left alone for too long; nor will it help the housetraining process.

Don't Punish After the Fact

Be prepared for your puppy to have accidents in the house. It happens to even the best trainers! If you do actually catch him in the act of eliminating in the house, immediately say, "Out," then pick him up and take him outside, where hopefully he will finish (if you're lucky). Remain calm and try not to become overly excited or angry. Praise him while he is finishing outside, but don't worry if he doesn't finish. The quickness of rushing him out the door when he is in the process of relieving himself is sending him a message. Remember: He does not yet know the rules, and chances are it was your fault for not getting him out sooner.

We highly recommend that you purchase a dog crate for your new puppy.

If your puppy has an accident in the house, and you do not catch him, it is simply too late. Punishing the puppy for something he did a few minutes or even seconds ago will not make sense to him. Punishing after the fact will only teach your puppy that your behavior is sometimes unpredictable, causing him not to trust you. Just clean up the soiled area with an enzymatic cleaner (there are many products on the market designed for this purpose that you can purchase at your local pet store), and tell yourself to do a better job at supervising the puppy next time.

The Crate

We highly recommend that you purchase a dog crate for your new puppy, ideally one that will be big enough for him when he is grown. Think of the crate as the puppy's bedroom. It should be a comfortable, dry, warm, safe place for him to rest.

You need to determine where you will put the crate. What room will the puppy be in at night? Many puppies do best if they can sleep in their crate in your bedroom, rather than being left alone in another room or in the basement. The puppy has just left the only home he has ever known, where he slept with possibly four to seven littermates. Now he is alone in

The crate—your puppy's home away from home.

your home with you. It's important that the pup finds comfort in knowing that you are close by. If you cannot fit the crate in your bedroom or choose not to have the puppy sleep there, where will you put it? Keep in mind that you will want to be able to hear him and know when he gets up during the night, since that's often a sign that he needs to go out.

Safe Haven

The crate should be a safe haven for the puppy, where he can feel comfortable and secure and not be bothered. It is a place where he can go to get away from the excitement and commotion that might be caused by the kids and their visiting friends. If used properly, a puppy will go into the crate on his own for a rest and when he needs a break. You must teach your children that the crate is for the puppy, not a fort or a hideout that they can crawl in and out of. When the puppy is in his crate, they should not disturb him. This includes poking at the puppy, or kicking and banging the crate. Do not permit your children to put food or other items through the crate bars, since they can end up giving the puppy something that might be dangerous to him.

Children must also be taught never to open the crate door if you have put the puppy there for safekeeping. It can sometimes be upsetting for young children to see a puppy in a cage—they feel the need to let him out. Explain to them that the crate is the puppy's home or bedroom, and that he is happy and comfortable there. If a child lets a puppy out of his crate and you are unaware, it could be disastrous.

KEEP IN MIND

Just Trying to Help

Lynn's children were fascinated by their puppy being in the crate, and often felt the need to "set him free." She constantly heard, "But mommy, he wants to get out!" One day, Pia and Lynn were at an outdoor dog show with both puppies and both of Lynn's children. The puppies were 3 months old. It was a nice day and, while setting up for a picnic lunch by the minivan, the back hatch of the van was open with the puppies in their crates. Moments later, Lynn's 4-year-old son climbed into the back of the van and opened a crate door—out popped a puppy! Pia and Lynn turned around in astonishment to see one of their puppies having a great time running in the grass. Luckily, they were able to get the puppy back to them with little trouble and all was well; but what if a car had come by? What if the puppy had run over to an unfriendly dog at the show? Any number of things could have happened. When Lynn asked her son why he had opened the crate to let the puppies out, his reply was, "They wanted to be part of our picnic. I was just trying to help, mommy."

Size of the Crate

The size of the crate will depend upon the size of your puppy. To save you time and money, purchase a crate that will be big enough for your puppy when he is full grown. There should be enough room so that your puppy can comfortably lie in one half and, *only if absolutely necessary*, urinate or defecate in the other half. Obviously, you want to avoid this so the puppy doesn't get into the habit of soiling in his crate, but it's better than having the crate too small, forcing the puppy to lie in his own excrement. Because of this, the crate is a valuable tool to aid in the housetraining process.

You can try putting something soft and dry in one half of the crate, like an old towel, for the puppy to lie on. You may not want to purchase an expensive puppy bed at this stage, since it may get chewed. You also do not want to

**Make sure
that the puppy's
time in the crate
is not excessive.**

cover the entire crate bottom with bedding. If the puppy needs to eliminate and cannot possibly hold it any longer, and you are not there to let him out, he will hopefully go in the area that is not covered with the bedding that he likes to sleep on. Keep in mind that if you are getting your puppy out frequently, putting him on a schedule, and paying attention to when he needs to go, your puppy may never have an accident in the crate. That should be your goal.

When to Use the Crate

Use your puppy's crate whenever you cannot supervise him. You will know that he is safe in the crate, and the house will be safe from him. When the puppy is in the crate, you can give him an appropriate, safe chew toy to occupy his time. If you must leave him there for a long period of time, you

You can give your puppy a safe chew toy while he is in the crate.

might want to leave water for him as well. *Please make sure that the puppy's time in the crate is not excessive*. He needs to have sufficient time for play, exercise, and human interaction, and also to investigate and experience the different rooms of the house while you are there watching him. We have seen instances where owners have kept their puppies constantly crated or confined to a single room while in the house, never allowing them to go in to the other rooms for fear that the puppy will have an accident, chew something, or become too rambunctious and "annoy" the family. These puppies become very frustrated and, once let out of their crate or barrier, they do end up running around crazily, filled with the excitement of being in the forbidden rooms.

Our puppies were always uncrated when we were in the house with them. They were encouraged to go from room to room *with us*—no room was off limits. We made sure that they received sufficient exercise outside to help tire them, so they could be calm and relaxed in the house. The end result is two adolescent dogs who can be loose in the house, and will, on their own, move from room to room with us simply because that's what they are used to. They will also, on their own, go into their crates to rest.

Housetraining takes time, a commitment on your part, and understanding that your puppy does not know any better until you teach him. He must learn where to eliminate, and it's up to you to show him. It will probably take several months to have a truly reliably housetrained dog. Keep in mind that all puppies are different in the amount of time it will take, and some will be easier to train than others. Most important, your puppy's success greatly depends on your efforts.

Section 3

Interacting With Your Puppy

Chapter 8

Communicating with Your Dog and Understanding Body Language

Your adorable new puppy is in your home, and you realize as he is running through the house that he is not listening to a word you say. How do you interact with this nonhuman member of your family? The important thing to remember, no matter how much you love your puppy and would like to treat him as an additional child, is that he is still a canine, not a furry little person. In order to learn how to communicate with your puppy, you will need to know what your body language and voice conveys to the puppy. Let's start first with getting an understanding of communication.

Communication

Communication is an exchange of information. It requires a sender, a message, and a receiver. The signal sent must be clear to both parties to avoid causing anxiety and conflict. Since communication is a learned behavior, the important thing to realize is that it is not so much what we *say*, but what the receiver of the message *hears*. When our signals are crossed, or the message sent is not heard or understood, the result is typically frustration by one of the parties.

Imagine going to a foreign country where you do not speak the language and have no understanding of their customs. You are lost, and decide to stop at a farmhouse. The

Imagine how difficult it is for your dog to understand you.

farmer waves to you to come into his home. As you step into the house, the farmer quickly turns his head and gives you a dirty look—you are unaware that the proper etiquette of the country is to remove your shoes before entering a house. The farmer begins talking to you in an enraged tone of voice, flailing his arms in the air, but you have no idea what he is saying. He is outraged; you are shocked; both of you are perplexed. Your behavior was inappropriate, but how would you know? Imagine how difficult it is for your dog to understand you.

When communication is misinterpreted, not heard, or unclear between people and dogs, both parties become confused. Many times, the outcome will result in the development of behavioral problems. When a dog is frustrated and bewildered, he will try other behaviors in an attempt to see what works best to thwart the tension. Many of these behaviors may not be tolerable to you. Let's go over a very typical scenario.

Your children have been sneaking food to your puppy from the dinner table for several months. You have been reprimanding them, warning that the puppy will eventually get big enough to jump up and reach the food from the table. As surmised, the puppy is rapidly growing and now jumping up onto the table and stealing food from the children's plates. The puppy has, up to this point, been encouraged to hang around the dinner table, since there has always been something in it for him. Now, everyone is scolding the puppy for the same behavior he has been rewarded for over the past few months. Since the food is more rewarding than the few reprimands, the puppy sits tight in hopes of a juicy steak bone. You get up for a drink and the pup sees an opportunity for a reward, so he jumps up and steals the bone from your plate. Now everyone is angry, and the puppy is banned from the kitchen or put into a crate. The upset puppy begins to bark in his crate (a nuisance behavior). Your scolding turns into yelling, and your quiet dinners have now turned into turmoil. What started off as an innocent behavior (hanging around the table) was unintentionally rewarded (feeding from the table) and turned into a behavior problem.

Dog Communication

Every interaction that you have with your dog consists of some form of communication sent by you and received by your dog and vice versa. When you praise and pet your dog for a job well done, you are communicating your approval of the dog's behavior. If praising and petting are rewarding to your dog, he should show signs of happiness.

Dogs do not continue to do things if they aren't rewarding to them.

Your dog will communicate things to you as well. Your dog might signal that he wants something from you. For example, he may scratch at the back door, signaling that he needs to relieve himself. If you open the door every time he scratches at it, the dog learns that the action of scratching at the door will cause someone to open it, thus giving him an opportunity to relieve himself. Or, your dog may drop a ball in your lap when he wants to play. If you toss it, then the dog learns that dropping a ball into your lap elicits play. If you don't toss it, dropping a ball in your lap has no meaning, and he will stop that action. Dogs do not continue to do things if they aren't rewarding to *them*.

Your dog might also attempt to communicate when he does *not* want something from you, or to cease what you are doing. For example, your dog might growl at your children when they attempt to move him from the sofa. He is communicating that he doesn't want to be bothered at this moment.

What Is Your Dog's Body Language Saying?

As you know, people primarily communicate through vocalization. We certainly do use body language as well, but we primarily communicate by speaking. Dogs communicate by using three techniques:

- olfactory (scent or smell through urine marking, anal gland expression, etc.)
- visual (body postures, facial expressions, etc.)
- auditory (vocalizations, e.g., barking, whining, whimpering, yelping, howling)

If you want to learn to read your dog, pay close attention to his face.

This makes the task of dogs and humans communicating with one another a rather difficult one; often, miscommunication will be the result of one or the other's efforts. You need to do your homework in order to prevent misunderstandings. Let's look at some typical dog body language.

Facial Expressions and Tail Position

Dogs display many different facial expressions. If you want to learn to read your dog, pay close attention to his face, especially his ears, mouth, lips, and eyes. Also pay attention to his tail. Take a good look at your dog when he is at home, comfortable and relaxed, with nothing around to cause stress or excitement, and notice how he carries his ears and tail. They are the most noticeable and easiest to read body parts. Learn what a relaxed position is for these body parts—then you will be able to notice when they change.

Ears

Changes in your dog's ears are usually easy to notice. Whether your dog has erect upright ears or floppy ears, they will change position based on how the dog feels. If the dog has become aroused or very excited, the ears are forward and up high on the head (this also occurs in an offensive-aggressive or threatening dog). If the ears are low on the head and perhaps flattened and moved slightly backward, it is usually a sign of a friendly or submissive dog. Ears that are really flattened to the head and far backward are usually a sign that the dog may be very timid or fearful. If the threat gets too close, the dog may make a defensive aggressive or threatening posture toward the intruder.

Mouth and Lips

A dog may bare his teeth when he feels threatened. If the dog is warning in an offensive manner, the dog's lips are retracted vertically and the canine teeth may be visible. If the dog is warning in a defensive manner, the lips are horizontal from the corners of his mouth, and you will see more teeth than in the offensive threat. An often misinterpreted facial expression is what is called a submissive grin. Here, the dog lifts the front part of his lips exposing his teeth, but it is important to notice the dog's eyes and body movements. The eyes are usually squinting and the rest of his body is either relaxed or wiggly. This is a nonthreatening gesture.

Tail

A dog's tail is also one of the more noticeable body parts that changes based on what the dog is feeling. A tail that is raised and carried high is a sign of an aroused dog; and a tail that is carried very low, possibly even

It is very helpful to be able to read your puppy's facial expressions.

between the back legs, is a signal to you that your dog is not comfortable in the present situation and even becoming fearful.

Some people believe that a wagging tail is a positive signal, but this is a huge misconception. We have heard from many people that a dog bit someone when his tail was wagging. A friendly dog will wag his tail at a rapid speed, and many times his rear end is moving side to side. A dog who is feeling threatened or is threatening will wag his tail more slowly, and his body posture will be more stiff.

Eyes and Stares

A dog's facial expressions are important to read. A change in your dog's eyes can be difficult to notice, such as the pupils becoming dilated. This will

Be sure to pay close attention to your dog as he interacts with different people.

often happen when the dog is highly aroused, frightened, or agitated. But one thing to be aware of regarding the eyes is that direct prolonged staring is considered threatening to the dog, and will often result in a fight or bite if the threat does not back away. When a dog is feeling threatened, his body may be very still but he might give you a look out of the corner of his eyes. You may only see the whites of his eyes (sometimes called whale eye). Be careful if you see this, since the dog is in an offensive state of mind.

General Body Postures

A dog on the offensive typically stands tall with his head held high, his ears and tail high and forward, and his weight is on his front feet, facing whatever it is that has alerted him. A dog on the defensive has a lower, cowered down body posture, with most of the weight backward rather than forward, his head held down and slightly turned away. His ears will likely be back and his tail down. Many times, the dog will crouch; however, he can quickly dart forward.

There are many subtle variations on the different body positions mentioned above, but these are the easiest to learn to read. Be sure to pay close attention to your dog as he interacts with different people. Is he giving any signals that he might be uncomfortable by the approach of a certain person? Perhaps it is when children approach, or maybe tall men, or people with hats and sunglasses on. If you know that these situations cause your dog to become uncomfortable or nervous, it can help you to avoid problems and obtain help to try to work him through it.

Dogs Greeting Dogs

Observe two dogs who do not know one another, approaching each other off leash in a park. They will begin to check one another out at some distance away. Each is observing the body language of the other dog. What is the other saying with his body? Is he approaching in a friendly manner? Does he look cautious, timid, or afraid? Is he moving in a forceful, aggressive manner? As they trot toward one another, they will pause briefly at each other's face for a quick sniff. Some dogs may lick or nudge the other's face during the initial greeting. If one dog rests his head, chin, or neck over the other dog's shoulder area, or places his front paws on the shoulder of another, this would be

This is a polite dog greeting.

taken as a threat, and may end up in a fight. Not all dogs will greet mouth to mouth, but most do.

In a friendly dog greeting, after the brief contact at the head, the two dogs will move toward the rear of the other dog to sniff that dog's hindquarters or anal area. Dogs do this in order to determine the sex of the other dog, to check if the dog is familiar, and to discern if the other dog is anxious. Many people discourage dogs from greeting, since they feel the dog is being "rude" when he begins to sniff the anal area of the other dog, but this is proper canine greeting and should *not* be discouraged. If your dog is greeting another dog on leash, be sure to keep the leash very loose to give the dogs ample opportunity to flee if they feel uncomfortable. Far too many people make the leash taut so the dogs have no freedom of movement, and this can have a huge impact on the greeting and the outcome.

Compare this dog greeting to a polite, proper greeting between two people. Most likely it would be to approach the other person, verbally introduce themselves, and hold out their hand to shake the hand of the other person. We must keep in mind that dogs do not speak to one another in the sense that we do.

A greeting between two people who are good friends would look different from strangers greeting each other. They may walk right up to one another and immediately hug closely and even kiss. The handshake and verbal introduction is not needed. A greeting between dogs who are very familiar and friendly with one another is just as different. One dog might bark excitedly at the sight of another dog whom he knows and likes. Two dogs who know one another well may run right up and immediately start jumping, tackling, and wrestling with each other. It is very impolite and considered bad manners for your puppy to run up to a strange dog and jump on top of him, even if he is friendly; they do not know one another yet. This could cause the dog being jumped on to become afraid or defensive. Imagine walking up to a total stranger on the street and jumping on top of them, wrapping your arms and legs around him. What happens next is probably not going to be pleasant.

Dogs have many different styles of play.

Dog Play Styles

Dogs have many different styles of play. Some dogs are more physical than others and like to wrestle, tackle, and body slam one another and roll around on the floor. Other dogs do not like as much physical interaction and prefer to play chase games instead. Many dogs, when chasing, will try to stop or catch their play partner by using their mouths. Some dogs will also change their play style based on the preference of the dog they are playing with. A common friendly gesture that you may have seen dogs perform is what we call a play bow. The dog will stretch backwards, lowering his front half so his elbows are almost on the ground, and his rear end is up high in the air. Sometimes they will pounce themselves into this position in a silly, fun manner. It is used to invite and encourage another dog to play, and says to the other dog that he's looking to have some fun. Pawing at the other dog and twisting the body are also done during play situations.

Personal Space

Most animals (and even humans) have an area of personal space that surrounds them. It is the distance between them and another animal or person where they feel comfortable. For some dogs, this space might be 20 feet when strangers approach before the dog moves away. For another dog, the stranger may get within 5 feet before the dog leaves. And for other dogs the stranger may be able to walk right up to them. When a dog's, personal space is invaded, he has several choices: fight, flee (also

Wrestling and having fun.

called flight), freeze, fidget, or faint (the latter is quite rare). The two most common are flight, where the dog may choose to move away (if he can) from whatever makes him uncomfortable, or he may choose to fight, and try to make the thing causing the discomfort leave.

So, how do we get along and co-exist together with this animal living in our homes, who does not understand the form of communication that we use most comfortably—speech? Your puppy was not born understanding human language. Trying to communicate with your puppy by speaking to him is like trying to communicate with someone from another country who does not speak or understand your language. To effectively speak to your puppy, you much teach the puppy that you expect a certain behavior in response to the different words you say to him. We'll discuss how to teach these desired behaviors and avoid problems in the following chapters.

Chapter 9

How Do Children Interact with Puppies, and How Should They?

Now that you know what your dog's body is saying in dog language, you can use that knowledge to help you communicate with your dog and avoid problems. What is your body language saying to your dog? More important, what is your child's body language saying?

There is a big difference between the way adults behave and move compared to young children. Children are much more unpredictable in their movements. They might be walking through the house and then suddenly start running. Young toddlers could be walking along and, for no apparent reason, suddenly fall. Children's arms tend to move differently as well. They are often more active and in motion than adults arms. They do not have a concept of personal space and will get very close to your face to tell you something. They are also noisy—they cry more often and let out shrieking screams of joy and excitement when playing. For many puppies, these little people can be quite disconcerting. It is hard enough for dogs to figure out adult human body language, but add children to the mix and it makes for a much more difficult time for the dog. It's not hard to see why dogs get confused, angry, or afraid.

Proper approach by a child. Also, teach your children to always ask for permission before approaching a dog.

Approaching the Puppy

Remember how friendly dogs approach other dogs? They trot in a relaxed manner toward the other dog and stop to sniff briefly at the dog's face. The casual, comfortable movement of the oncoming dog helps the dog being approached to relax. Now think about how children usually move. Not with calm, controlled, relaxed movements! When you approach a friendly dog, you should walk calmly (not overly slow or hesitant) at a normal pace toward the dog. Teach your children how to approach a dog. Stand upright and walk calmly toward the dog. Please teach your children that they should *always ask for permission* to approach a strange dog. Not all dogs like people, especially unfamiliar children.

A common expression of friendliness by a child is to approach a dog in a bent over posture with an arm extended outward. For many dogs, the leaning-over action makes them very uncomfortable, even when done by familiar people such as close family members. When dogs lean over other dogs, as discussed earlier, it is seen as a threatening or controlling gesture.

You are also invading their personal space. It is important to know that many dogs become frightened and will cower or back away when a person approaches in that manner. With puppies, it can help make the puppy more comfortable if the person squats straight down toward the ground in their own space (*not bending over the puppy*).

Discourage Running

Most children who like dogs will approach a dog in a manner that is quick and forceful looking. They often run toward them with open arms. For a puppy who is not used to children, this can be quite scary, especially if there is more than one child approaching. The puppy may be thinking, "Good grief, are they going to attack me?" Also, a sudden approach of a child running in from another room can scare or excite the puppy. The child's intention may not even be to approach the puppy, but the puppy doesn't know that. It's even worse and more startling for the puppy if he was sleeping or resting. The puppy becomes scared and runs away with the child running after him, or the puppy gets so excited he chases the child, and tries to stop the child by jumping on him, knocking him over, or grabbing the child's waving arms with his mouth. Try to discourage your children from running in the house, and make sure the puppy is getting adequate exercise to help keep him tired and content and less likely to join in the chase.

Teach your children that they should always ask for permission to approach a strange dog.

Touching and Petting

Why is it that when a child attempts to do something as simple as pet a puppy, they can often end up being mouthed (where the puppy puts his mouth and teeth on the child's hand, arm, etc.)? Does this mean you have a bad, dangerous, or out-of-control puppy? Not likely.

When adults pet a puppy, they calmly put their hand out for the puppy to sniff, and then touch the puppy. When children attempt to pet puppies, typically their hands start off very high up in the air and move downward, cautiously and slowly, almost dangling over the top of the puppy's head. There may even be a slight hesitation on the approach of the hand toward the puppy, as if they are thinking, "I want to pet the puppy, but I'm a bit unsure." The slow, hesitant hand motion causes most puppies to reach their heads up to meet the hand. As soon as children see the puppy's head and mouth

Help the child learn how to properly and calmly pet your puppy.

coming toward their hand, they immediately pull their hand higher away, sometimes making a screeching sound. This now excites the puppy and turns the petting attempt into a fun game (in the puppy's mind, anyway). It becomes an endless cycle of the hand going up and down and the puppy jumping up and down trying to grab the hand. The situation can quickly become out of control as the puppy becomes more and more aroused. It can turn a child's simple efforts to pet the puppy into the puppy's teeth on a hand or arm. This makes the child even more hesitant and worried about petting the puppy the next time.

The slight hesitation of a child's attempt to pet may also cause some puppies to react in a fearful manner, not trusting what the child's next move will be. This is especially true if the puppy is not accustomed to being around children. The puppy is probably thinking, "Is the hand going to touch me or not? Why is the hand moving in that manner?" A timid/shy puppy may back away, crouch down low, or avoid the child. In turn, the child may take a more aggressive approach, since the puppy is moving away. This can increase fear in the puppy, as well as cause the child to become frustrated. Try to avoid putting the puppy (and child) in these situations.

Teaching Children How To Pet

Teach children to start off with their hands low and relaxed by their side, bringing their hand toward the puppy's face at a normal pace, on a level plane with the puppy's head so the pup can sniff their hand.

They can then move their hand to touch the side of the puppy's face, neck, under the chin, or along the back. Most children need to be shown how to do this. Take hold of their hand and actually do the hand motion for them several times. If the puppy lies down, help the child calmly rub the puppy's belly area. If the hand approach is done properly, a well-mannered puppy will control himself and not put his mouth on the children's hands.

Very young toddlers do not know how to pet—they pat instead. Therefore, it is important to show them how to pat gently in order to avoid whacking the puppy. Try having them practice petting or patting one of their stuffed animals. This way, the stuffed animal can help the child through the learning stage, instead of your puppy.

Children who are not used to interacting with dogs are almost always leery of a dog's head (and the mouth with all those teeth coming toward them). Often, they reach out to pet a dog expecting to touch the nice soft fur on the body or back of the neck, only to find each time the dog's head turns toward their hand to check it out. Explain to children that the puppy wants to sniff, and possibly even lick or kiss their hand, so that they understand what to expect.

Pulling and Poking Are *Not* Part of Petting

It is important to explain to children that they should never pull any of the puppy's body parts, like the ears, tail, or long fur. These are not handles for holding on to, especially when the puppy is attempting to escape. Be aware that young toddlers are fascinated with things like the nose, eyes, ears, and mouth of the puppy. They will often try to touch the eyes with their fingers, put a finger up the puppy's nose or in the ears, and even try to touch and pull the puppy's tongue. It happens more often than you may think, so you must supervise any child who wants to pet your puppy. Do this for your puppy's sake as well as the child's.

Picking Up the Puppy

Most children want to pick puppies up and carry them around. Think about their own experiences—they were always being picked up by adults,

As a general rule, children should not pick up and carry puppies.

carried from place to place, and held. Probably being picked up was a pleasant experience for them. So, why wouldn't they want to do the same for the puppy? A puppy who's been picked up by a child may try to get free by fussing and wiggling in the child's arms, or mouthing the child's hands, causing the child to drop the puppy. Since children simply do not know how to properly pick up a puppy and are not aware that they might be hurting the puppy in the process, they should not be allowed to do so.

YOU'RE IN CHARGE

Supervise, Supervise, Supervise

Lynn's son had two friends over one day when their puppy was 9 weeks old. She supervised the children's greetings to the puppy, and then the kids started to play with one another and were no longer paying attention to the puppy. She turned her back for just a moment, only to hear a loud screech from the puppy. As she turned back around, she caught sight of the puppy being placed on the floor— one of the children had started to pick up the puppy and either hurt, startled, or scared him. If this type of behavior was allowed to continue, her puppy could have ended up being fearful and untrusting of children.

There is no reason for a child to ever pick a puppy up off the ground. Explain to them that this causes the puppy discomfort or pain. Find an explanation that your children can understand. Tell them that if they would like to hold the puppy, they should sit on the floor and you will help guide the puppy into their laps.

CASE STUDY

The Puppy Who Didn't Want to Be Picked Up

A family came to us with a 4-month-old Cockapoo puppy, Sandy, who they had since the puppy was 8 weeks old. The husband and wife explained that they were concerned about Sandy's behavior when they tried to reach down and pick her up. She used to be fine, but now she was becoming quite feisty and would growl and snap at their hands as they tried to grab her. After speaking with them, we found out that they had three young children in the house and that Sandy was constantly being picked up. She would be picked up to be put on the sofa, picked up to be taken off the sofa, picked up to be moved to their laps, picked up to be put on the floor or taken outside, picked up just to be held, etc. This poor puppy was picked up so frequently that, after this short period of time living with them, she was already telling them that she had enough!

Holding and Hugging

We love to hug and hold others, especially those we are fond of. It is a natural reaction for us to hold and hug our children, and we in turn teach and encourage them to perform this behavior. Our hugs help to express how much we care for our children and love them. Therefore, it is not surprising that children would want to do the same with their cute, fluffy puppy who they love so much. This behavior happens in young girls more so than boys.

Hugging and holding are very physical actions. For dogs, the use of physical force by one dog on another is usually done for control (as when one dog pins another dog down on the ground). This is not fun for the dog being held, or meant as a game. In play, one dog may end up on the ground with another on top of him, but if he wants to get up, the other dog will let him. That is not the case when one dog is holding another down to control him. Knowing this about dogs, what do you suppose your dog might think when your children are hugging him while lying on top of him? The children might be doing it just

What do you suppose your dog might think when your child hugs him and lies on top of him?

to snuggle with the dog, or maybe to wrestle with him (as is common with little boys). An older dog who is used to children might learn to tolerate this behavior from familiar children, however, it does not mean the dog likes it.

Warning Signals

A dog may not understand why the child is holding him. He may give a warning signal to let the child know that he does not like the behavior. This signal might be a struggle to get up, a curled, snarled mouth and lips, a growl or low grumble, or even snapping the mouth toward the child without making contact. If these warnings go unheeded, and the dog becomes more afraid, uncomfortable, or frustrated, he may resort to actually biting in order to get the child off him. Let's compare this to a confrontation between two people. If a stranger comes up to you very close in your face, you might first ask him to back away. If that does not work, you might try backing away. If the person moves closer to you and grabs your arm, you might push him away with your hand. If that does not work, you might scream, panic, or fight to get away. Warning signals escalate in severity. Many people will say that their dog bit with no warning; but this is not usually the case. The dog probably gave many warning signs, but no one recognized them or paid attention. Young children certainly will not recognize warning signals from a dog.

Young children will not recognize warning signals from a dog.

CASE STUDY

The Puppy Who Didn't Want to Be Held

Pia consulted with a client with two girls, Emily (age 8) and Leanne (age 11). They had a one-and-a-half-year-old male Shih Tzu named Winston. Winston was adopted by them at 6 months of age from a family with two toddler boys. Emily had been bitten in the face, on her lip, by Winston and required seven stitches. After much discussion with the family, it was determined that Emily held Winston a lot, more than any one else in the family. She loved him and wanted to hold him. If he was lying on the sofa or on the floor, she would sit next to him and hug him. The day of the bite was a bit more stressful than others for Winston because he had been to a new groomer. Emily's mom knew that Winston was not happy about his grooming experience when she picked him up. She said, "He just did not seem to be himself." Winston had already had enough of being handled by people that day. But, when he got home, instead of being able to rest and sleep it off, he had to deal with Emily's constant hugging. She thought he looked adorable with his new hair cut and could not resist. She sat next to him on the sofa, leaned over him, and began petting and hugging him. Winston had been giving warning signals (he attempted to move away, turned his body to face another direction, and curled his lip), but Emily did not understand them. Winston was becoming more annoyed and gave Emily an air snap (a snap toward her face with no intent to make contact). Emily backed away, startled, but wanted to convince Winston that she still loved him and went back to hugging him. Since his several warnings did not work, he decided to get his point across a bit more severely by biting her. Of course her face was right next to his, and she got bit on the lip. The mother was extremely upset by the bite and gave Winston a firm correction, long after the incident happened. From Winston's perspective, the adult whom he trusted had lost her mind—what in the world was she punishing him for? He was sleeping by the time she reprimanded him. Yet, we can't blame the parent. She was upset and concerned about her child's face and the prospect of having to get rid of the dog who they all loved so much.

Any time a dog bites a person, it is a horrible experience for all involved. Unfortunately, when dogs bite children it is often in the face, which can be even more frightening and scarring (both physically and mentally) for the child. Children get bit in the face because their faces are usually close to the dog, especially during hugging and holding episodes. A dog and a child left alone together for even one minute could result in a serious problem for the child, the dog, or both.

A dog may be able to tolerate one hug from a child, but constant touching and restraining may be uncomfortable, frightening, or just plain annoying for the dog. Some dogs may view a child's hug as a threatening gesture.

Roughhousing, Wrestling, and Tackling

These types of physical interactions tend to foster combative behaviors between children and dogs, which typically result in some form of competition where there is a winner and a loser. Many children watch wrestling on television and most boys will, sometime in their lives, be involved in some form of roughhousing, tackling, or other rough sport. The goal of a wrestling match is to pin the opponent; in a football game it is to tackle the runner with the ball. Most dogs will quickly tire of these activities and give signals that they've had enough. While adults may be able to distinguish when enough is enough, children cannot. Therefore, avoid these types of interactions at all costs. There is no reason to interact with a dog in this manner.

Screaming, Crying, and Temper Tantrums

Children vocalize when they need or want something. Depending upon the age of your child, it can vary from whining, begging, screaming, crying, or, thankfully, calmly asking. When the noise level in a household goes up, the level of anxiety and arousal does as well. Think about a child's birthday party or Christmas morning when children are opening gifts. The activity and noise level is much higher than normal. After a while, the high-pitched voices of children may even start to get on your nerves. If it gets on your nerves, think how much it can affect your puppy. Not only is the puppy feeding off your stress, but he is also feeding off the energy of the children. Some pups may find this noise level so difficult to deal with that groups of children end up becoming threatening to him. Yes, children are children, but the more you can control the noise level in the home, the better. If possible, sending the children to a playroom or outdoors can help the puppy calm down (and settle your nerves at the same time).

The more you can control the noise level in the home, the better.

When children feel frustrated, angry, hurt, or disappointed, they often express themselves by having a temper tantrum. They may begin to cry, scream, lie on the floor and kick their feet or stomp up and down. Temper tantrums (typically between the ages of 1 and 3) are a normal part of a child's development as he learns self-control. Temper tantrums are a way for your child to let off steam. Add a puppy into the picture during this developmental stage of your child, and you may have your hands full. Your child may have a tantrum out of frustration because most puppies simply do not listen to children, especially those under the age of 6. As a parent, you can sometimes tell when tantrums are coming. Your child may seem moody, cranky, or difficult. Try to remove the puppy from the picture, if possible, or distract the child away from the puppy. Hitting, kicking, throwing things, or prolonged screaming and yelling around the puppy should not be tolerated. A time out for the child may be in order to keep the puppy safe and ensure that he isn't becoming frightened of your child and mistrusting his or her actions.

Teach your children that puppies are delicate and must be handled properly.

Crawling Infants

An infant crawling on the floor can be quite interesting to a puppy or young dog. An infant, whether lying on the floor or crawling, is in the perfect position to be checked out by the dog, including being jumped on, walked over (both of which could hurt the baby), licked, and sniffed. Your dog may view a crawling baby as a playmate; this could result in the dog putting his mouth on the baby or pawing at the baby with his sharp nails. We have talked about how difficult it must be for the dog to understand our body language and that of our children. A crawling infant brings about a third challenge for the dog. They do not likely view infants the same way as they view young children who are at a walking age. A crawling infant is on the dog's level, and may crawl right over to his food dish while he is eating, or crawl up to him while he is chewing on his favorite bone. The child appears to be a threat, and the dog may feel the need to protect these valuable items. When one dog is about to challenge another dog, the challenger might get into a low crouched position (similar to a stalking position), make direct eye contact with the other dog, and slowly move toward the dog to be challenged, staring the entire way. An infant crawling toward a dog probably has a similar appearance, even though we know the infant's intent is not a challenge. Therefore, *constant supervision is a must* when you have an infant and a dog in the house. Do not take chances and assume that the two will get along fine. Always use common sense and a "better safe than sorry" attitude.

Constant supervision is a must when you have an infant and a dog in the house.

Adolescent Play

As children begin to mature, their play styles obviously change. Many adolescent children engage in competitive and/or combative play games where the focus might be on win/lose with an attitude of "I'm in charge." While adolescent children have more control over themselves and their movements, their desire to control the dog or win the game can affect the relationship. We highly encourage you to get your child involved in a training class or 4-H Club with your dog. This will help teach the child how to gain control over the dog without force and to ensure they continue to interact with one another in an appropriate, respectful manner.

Incorporating training into the play sessions is invaluable. For example, if your child is tugging with the dog, the child should teach the dog to relinquish the toy when asked, sit or lie down between tug sessions, and only take the toy when told. Now your child is controlling the game, and both are having a grand time.

Puppies Are Delicate

Children must learn that puppies are delicate, much like babies. They frighten easily, become startled by quick sudden movements, and can become injured by falling, being knocked over, stepped on, or accidentally kicked. Please help to guide and teach your children how to properly conduct themselves around puppies and how to handle a dog of any age or size. Remember that your puppy should not have to tolerate constant contact, handling, or abuse by children.

Some dogs are more tolerant of children than others. If at any time you are not comfortable with something that your dog is doing, and you are not sure whether he is displaying a friendly gesture or a threatening one, always consult a professional in the field.

Chapter 10

Playing with Puppies

It makes little sense to try to convince your 5-year-old that puppies are not motorized toys. It makes even less sense to persuade your 10-week-old puppy that your children are not little creatures who need to be chased after and played with like stuffed toys. On the other hand, there is nothing more heartwarming than looking at a child curled up into a little ball with a sleeping, content puppy, or seeing the two playing in unison, as equal playmates, both enjoying the interaction. But you will never be able to enjoy these scenes if your child and puppy are not taught how to walk down the path of harmony together.

Interacting and playing with dogs can certainly enhance children's self-esteem, teach them responsibility, help them learn about empathy, and enjoy the bond that people have with their canine friends. Yet you should never assume that your children know how you want them to behave around or interact with your puppy (and vice versa). That assumption will set up both puppy and child to fail. Your puppy has no understanding how children are supposed to be treated, especially during play sessions when everyone is aroused; nor do your children have an understanding how to treat a puppy, unless you teach them how to properly interact with one another. Puppies can be opportunistic—ruled by their instincts, not "right and wrong." And even when the puppy and child have an understanding of the rules that you have established, it doesn't mean they will necessarily obey them all of the time.

Perhaps one day your puppy and child are overexuberant because they have been forced to stay indoors on account of the weather. Both lack sufficient exercise and have had no outlet to get rid of their pent-up energy. As a result, no one is following the rules of play that you have tried to establish. Your child loses all self-control and has an outburst. The puppy losses self-control and begins biting and jumping up at the child as the child's vocalization increases. No one is having fun, especially you. This does not make for good playmates or help you maintain your sanity.

The key factor is to look at every child as an individual and work with his abilities or interest. To make a generalization that children understand what they can and cannot do with puppies is just setting you up for disappointment and failure.

CASE STUDY
The Trouble with Roughhousing

A mom consulted with Pia regarding her son Tommy and his behavior toward their puppy. She felt he was not listening to her, even after making many attempts to explain to him how he should play with the new puppy. She was *right*! When observing Tommy and the puppy interacting, Pia's heart went out to the pup. The play session looked like a World Wrestling Federation bout—out of control—and the puppy was treated like an object. (The only difference was no one was cheering for a winner.) One or the other was going to get hurt. The biggest concern was that the puppy would eventually bite the boy or another child, if this conduct continued. Tommy had a difficult time understanding responsibility, had little or no empathy for the puppy, and the bond was deteriorating quickly.

It turns out, whenever Tommy was visiting with his father (who had an adult dog), the father encouraged this kind of roughhouse play, since this is how Dad played with his adult dog. During the session with Tommy, Pia mimicked what he was doing to the pup by treating him like he treated the pup. Soon he realized how the play session felt to the puppy. Tommy was now willing to listen to her suggestions. Since boys and girls play differently (see below), to expect him to play with the pup in a soft, tender way was useless. This young boy had to be taught how to play with this puppy like a well-mannered boy. We had to find a motivation for him to stick to the rules.

Tommy was shown some fun games, and they came up with silly names for tricks that made him giggle and roll on the floor with laughter. She now had his attention and was ready to work. They started to work on passive-puppy behaviors such as "down," but they decided to call it "splat." With every successful "splat" he got from the pup, they gave each other a high-five, and his reward was shadow boxing with Pia (not the puppy). Tommy's reward would end if he got too rough or touched Pia (impulse control). Eventually, the puppy was told to "splat" and "freeze" (stay) during their high-five and shadow boxing game. Tommy then gave the pup a treat and released him by tossing a ball. He was learning to get his pup to be calm and still; the pup was learning to watch him from a passive position when Tommy was active, without getting aroused himself. There was to be no physical contact between the two unless the boy was nicely petting the pup, and the pup was responding to the boy's cues and not biting at the boy. Soon, Tommy was proud to show off his tricks to dad, and wanted to teach the adult dog the same tricks.

Dog Play

Puppies weren't born understanding the behaviors of people, especially children. Through observation and interaction, they slowly learned about us, both good and bad. People tend to think that the puppy sees their children as littermates. While on the surface this may appear to be true, it is not. They realize that children are a different species, yet their behaviors are very different than the taller humans (adults). Since children's behaviors are immature and playful by nature, puppies tend to become stimulated by their actions and antics. Think about when you get on the floor with your puppy and behave in a manner in which only those near and dear to you will ever be permitted to see. The puppy becomes excited and usually begins jumping, grabbing, holding on to clothing, and eventually the interaction gets out of control if not stopped before the puppy is too aroused. This is very similar to what puppies do with their littermates during play. They are simply playing like dogs with us, as they did with their littermates. This is how dogs play, regardless of whether it is with a child or dog.

Play is a valuable aspect of dog behavior.

Dog trainers can spend hours observing puppies and dogs playing with one another. Once you have an understanding of canine body language and social behavior, well-socialized dogs playing together can look like a ballet. As we discussed in Chapter 1, play begins very early in a puppy's life. Puppies learn a lot in the litter through play interactions. They can negotiate dominance and subordinance, they learn about strength, speed, agility, and more.

Play is a valuable, important aspect of dog behavior and much more comprehensive than is generally acknowledged. Puppies offer many appeasement behaviors, which they learn very early on when they are playing with their littermates. These behaviors serve an important role in the dog's ability to have well-rounded social interactions with others. Playful interactions continue as a result of trust, tolerance, and understanding boundaries, rules, and the ability to exhibit inhibition with their mouths. Incorporated within play are fun, attention, affection, combative skills, emotional control, and risks. It is critical that you give your puppy as many opportunities to play as you can, not only with other sociable puppies or adult dogs, but also with adults and children.

As we observed our puppies grow into the adolescent phase, their play styles changed. When play is plentiful during puppyhood, they gain skills and learn to cope with various situations. When a puppy feels comfortable with another puppy or dog, the pup will perform a posture that invites the other to play, called a play bow. The dog's front elbows are resting on the

Finding an agility class in your area can be a fun outlet.

ground while the back end is in the air. There is a momentary pause, and then the pup will jump up into the air with glee.

Through play, puppies learn much about their abilities and limits. Incorporating obstacles into the play session helps the puppy develop confidence and increases his ability to use various parts of his body in different ways. When puppies jump over, crawl under, or run around objects, it can help them learn to solve or resolve problems later in life. An owner might think his dog is dumb because, for example, the dog can't figure out how to back out from behind the cocktail table when one side is blocked off. No, this dog isn't dumb, he simply didn't learn to problem solve around obstacles during puppyhood. Taking your puppy to a puppy agility class (similar to that of a playground and obstacle course for children) is highly recommended—and it's fun for both of you. If you can't find an agility class in your area, you can have fun by taking your puppy on hikes through the woods and teaching him to jump over fallen trees; or perhaps to the beach walking on the sand, running in and out of the water.

Dogs love to play—it seems to be self-motivating and self-rewarding. Isolating your puppy from having opportunities to play will have a negative impact on him later in life. Many people will say that their dog doesn't like to play. This is a sad statement. When you see these dogs, it's not so much that they don't *like* to play, but they don't know *how* to play. Through play, they learn about dog and human body language, how to compromise, learn about give-and-take, and much more. Don't deprive them of this important aspect in life.

It is critical that you give your puppy as many opportunities to play as you can.

Comparing Dog and Child Play

Similarities of Play

By 6 months of age, infants begin to use their limbs in various manners such as grasping, holding, pushing, grabbing, and more. According to Jean Piaget in *Play, Dreams, and Imitations in Childhood*, as children age, their motor skills develop and they become more coordinated. They create more complex sequences in their play styles. For example, instead of simply pushing a ball, the child may push the ball and crawl to it. As time goes on, the child pushes the ball, crawls to it, picks it up, and tosses it. This can be compared with puppies and retrieving. Like children, puppies gradually learn to chain behaviors together as well. They might initially run after the ball, yet do nothing once they get there. (In fact, many people tell us that their puppy likes to retrieve, but doesn't bring the object back. We always chuckle, without malice of course, and ask what, in their mind, does retrieve mean? They typically laugh along with us.) As puppies age and learn, they might run after the ball and pick it up. As time goes on, you should have a complete retrieve: you toss the ball, he chases it, picks it up, runs it back to you, and drops it.

By the time the children are toddlers, their social skills begin to develop. They engage in play with others, and engage others to play with them. This is the time when the toddler will want to interact with the puppy as often as possible. This can be a trying time, since the games of the toddler can act like a competitive game to the puppy. Keep-away or take-away games are fun for toddlers, yet can be very frustrating for the puppy.

Toddlers can change from day to day. The sweet child who was playing so gently one day may turn into a bully the next. The key factor to recall is that children act mostly on impulse, as do puppies. If your child is beginning to exhibit bully-like behaviors, it is critical to supervise this child. A child should *never* be permitted to bully a puppy (and vice versa). Make sure you express your disapproval of the child's behavior, teach the child how to behave, and praise the child for any accomplishment or effort that you see.

A child should never be permitted to bully a puppy.

When children play, their movements are quick and jerky, and the tone of their voice is typically squealing and high pitched, especially when excited. They roll around on the ground, leap into the air, hang on to one another, and move quickly from room to room. Now, let's look at the behaviors of a puppy. They seem to be in constant motion, rarely, if ever, walk (unless they are tired or not feeling well), roll on the ground, leap into the air, and grab onto skin or the clothing of people. They may also bark in high-pitched tones when excited. Consequently, even though they are two different species, their play behaviors are quite similar. Then why wouldn't they get along without supervision during play? Simply, as we explained in Chapter 8, dogs speak "dog" and children speak "human."

Differences of Play

Although there are similarities in their play styles, there are differences as well. Children do not use their teeth during play (even though they go through a biting stage); puppies do. Children do not nip at other children's heels or grab at their clothing with their mouths; puppies do.

By the age of 5, children enjoy playing pretend games, and may incorporate them into formal games with peers. Pretend games can consist of

Puppies were not born in a hive.

role-play. Many girls like to play dress up with their dogs. In fact, when they were young, dress up was part of Pia's sister's daily play sessions with her girlfriends. But dogs know nothing about wearing outfits—your Tibetan Terrier puppy may not like playing the role of Cleopatra; or wearing Barbie's wigs may not be your Basset Hound's thing. (It always surprises us that dogs will accept or tolerate wearing sweaters, coats, and booties that we put on them in the winter.) This is not acceptable play. The children don't know how to dress dogs, and they may attempt to bend legs in the wrong direction and accidentally harm them.

Many boys may play war-like or spy games. Aiming weapons or tossing fake grenades at a puppy is certainly not acceptable play, and probably not the kind of play that the puppy enjoys. Think how much fun it is for some children, especially if they hit the target. Once again, the child is being a child and doesn't understand that this type of play cannot be conducted with a dog.

Individual Play Styles

Not only do puppies and children have different play styles, but children themselves will have different play styles. Play may vary according to the temperament of the child, the child's upbringing, gender, culture, and much more. Some children exhibit great flexibility during play, while others who prefer board games or solo fantasy play may not want a puppy present during play. Studies have found that the play of boys tends to be much more exploratory, and the play of girls more symbolic. Since boys' and girls' play styles are so different, it's very hard to make a blanket statement that a particular breed is good with children. It would be very hard for any breed of dog to be that flexible. It is unwise to think that every dog within a certain breed will be good with children—dogs are individuals as well. Some will be good with children, some will not.

Changing Play Styles

When you first bring your puppy home, you may need to encourage your children to change their play styles while indoors. If they want to play in a rough manner by running and screaming, then that type of play should be taken outdoors without the puppy present. As previously mentioned, it is best to establish a house rule that the children are not allowed to run in the house, and the dogs are not allowed to roughhouse together indoors—those are all outdoor activities. Your puppy needs to become comfortable around children who are calm first, before the noise and activity level goes through the ceiling. Once the puppy is acclimated to the children and gaining confidence, you can gradually include the puppy into the play sessions.

Supervising Play

If you have children, you probably didn't leave them alone in a room, sandbox, or in the backyard so they could figure out how to play with other children. You initially supervised them by taking them to the playground, beach, park, or other areas where children gathered. You sat on the bench and supervised them, to ensure that their behavior was polite, correct, and to make sure no one got hurt or upset. If they misbehaved in any way, you immediately interrupted and instructed them how to interact with their new friends. If they chose not to listen to your direction, then you probably gave them a time-out by removing them from the situation—a punishment for their lack of compliance. During those early years, unsupervised children could easily get out of control by throwing sand into another child's face, grabbing toys from a child, not sharing, or pushing them over when they became frustrated. The child allowed to do so was learning something— behaviors that should have been discouraged early on.

Just like with young children, we never recommend that people drop their puppies off at a neighbor's house to play unsupervised. They may be having fun, but if you are not supervising them, you don't know what kind of play the pups are learning.

CASE STUDY
Unattended Play Is Not a Good Idea

A client with a Golden Retriever puppy had decided to put up one electronic fence around both her and her neighbor's properties, since the neighbor had recently purchased a Lab puppy the same age as the Golden. What fun for them! The pups were allowed to play unattended for hours at a time. The naive owners felt they were doing the puppies a favor, since they got plenty of play and exercise and slept through the night. Since their play was unsupervised, it became over the top, and the children could not play with the dogs since the cute little pups turned into wild, out-of-control, independent dogs.

They never took the pups for a walk and didn't socialize them with other puppies, so the two pups bonded very quickly—more so to each other than to their owners. The owners realized that, because of all of this unsupervised time, their dogs no longer looked to them, and even worse, no longer needed them. They wanted to rectify the situation, so the owners tried taking the now 6-month-old dogs for a walk. Both dogs were anxious about being away from the security of their yard. They couldn't walk on leash since they had never experienced leash walking. Neither dog tolerated strange dogs— they barked and lunged on-lead, fearful of any new dog who tried to greet them. They understood each other's body language, but not the body language of other dogs. What started off as good intentions by the owners to get their dogs some playtime, ended in two dogs with behavior problems.

Rules for Puppies When Playing with Children

Puppies are required to have control when they play with children, and vice versa. Play can escalate into aggression if the puppy has not learned to control himself. Either puppy or child may be injured as a result. As Dr. Karen London, an applied animal behaviorist so eloquently asked in a recent behavioral symposium at Tufts University on play behaviors, "Is the dog really exhibiting out-of-control play, or is the dog really out of his own control?"; "Is the play really out of control, or does the dog not know how to control himself?" All of this must be taken into consideration when you observe children and dogs playing together.

Play should be interrupted if the puppy does not follow the rules. You can easily teach the rules to your puppy by immediately intervening and stopping the session. The puppy will start to learn that his last action caused the fun to end, which is not what he wants. If he avoids that action/behavior, the fun continues. Here is a list of some rules that we teach parents to enforce when their children are playing with the puppy.

No Teeth on Children

If the puppy places his mouth on your child for any reason, the puppy should be removed from the session. Obviously, the child should not be encouraging this behavior. Fair is fair. The puppy should not be knocking them over, pulling at their clothing, or biting at them. Eventually, the puppy learns that each and every time he places his mouth on the child, the fun ceases.

Relinquish Objects When Told

If the child and puppy are playing with objects (e.g., balls, ropes) the puppy must learn to relinquish these objects when asked. If the puppy will not release the object, then play ends. (See the section in this chapter on how to teach your puppy to "give.")

Play should be interrupted if the puppy does not follow the rules.

Children Determine When Play Is Over, Not Puppies

This is an important factor in every play session, not only with children but adults. Many people say their puppy likes to play, but he goes about his business after a few minutes. If the puppy has learned early on that you and your children end the play sessions, not him, and you end it when the puppy is still interested in playing, then he will be even more interested in the play interaction. If you teach the puppy that he may stop when *he* wants to, he will probably decide when he would like play to start and stop throughout his life.

CASE STUDY
The Puppy Who Didn't Know How To Play

A pet sitter called recently and said she was having a difficult time exercising her client's 9-month-old intact male Boxer. The owners were away for 2 weeks, and this young dog needed more than a walk or two a day. The dog was quite dog friendly, but he had been permitted to play (unsupervised) at a doggy day care, resulting in very rough, bully-like play. It was difficult for the pet sitter to find a dog who could play with him since he intimidated most dogs he met. The owners used the day care as a means of giving the dog exercise, and never developed an exercise program that included them or the children. Now that the dog was home in the care of the pet sitter, the dog had no idea how to play with people, since he never learned about constructive play. The walks weren't enough, and she couldn't get the dog to run around or chase a ball. He was a handful, all because the owners took advantage of the offerings of the doggy day care, rather than taking on the responsibility to train the dog how to play with them at home when he was a puppy.

Puppies Must Obey Children

After you have taught your puppy some basic behaviors, such as sit, down, wait, and give, your children should be involved in the training. The age of the kids does not matter, as long as they are old enough to understand your direction. They should incorporate all of these commands during play sessions to maintain order and control. For example: The child throws the ball for the puppy. The puppy retrieves the ball and drops it at the child's feet. The child picks up the ball and, before throwing it again, asks puppy to sit. As a reward for sitting, the child throws the ball again.

Training helps develop respect.

Rules for Children and Games To Avoid

As we have reiterated in this book, training your puppy and child are critical to developing a healthy, respectful bond between the two. According to Steven Lindsay, "Good training is disciplined play." Parents must be careful to always control the intensity of play, especially with young puppies, to help them learn to control their direction, mouths, impulses, and promote deference. Like puppies, children are expected to follow rules as well. For example, children are expected to raise their hands before shouting out an answer in school. This is about controlling their enthusiasm and emotions. The same holds true when they play with puppies.

Use Positive Reinforcement During Play

Screaming, yelling, and reprimanding the puppy should not be part of play. Learning is not fun when someone attempts to scare us. Since you are teaching the puppy how to behave, screaming and yelling have no place in this process. Remain calm and teach your children to remain calm if things get out of control. You can have older children fill their pockets with treats and use treats as reinforcement when training for good behavior.

CASE STUDY
The Dog Who Liked To Tackle

The mother of six children phoned for some help with their 2-year-old Great Dane and her 6-year-old son. They were very good friends, yet the huge 150-pound male dog was tackling the boy and knocking him into trees when they played outside. This had been going on for 2 years. It would have been so much easier had she trained the dog when he was 10 pounds. We filled the boy's pockets with treats and had him run around the yard. Whenever the dog chased after him, he quickly turned to face the dog and said, "Sit." The dog sat and received treats. The boy then released him and ran around again. If the dog began chasing, the boy was to quickly tell him to sit or lie down and give treats after the dog obeyed. After a few lessons, the dog would chase the boy and when the boy turned to face him, instead of knocking him over, he would automatically sit or lie down.

Tug Games Must Be Supervised

While we are huge supporters of tug games, parents must be aware that overly aggressive tug games can encourage puppies to become overly aroused, confident, use their mouths harder, and develop some aggressive strategies. An older child playing tug with a young puppy could be strong enough to pick the puppy up off his feet while tugging. This could injure or frighten the puppy, or possibly cause him to become more aroused. Some puppies become aroused very easily and come flying at the tug toy with great force to grab it from your child's hand. They may miss the tug toy and grab your child's hand instead, or knock your child over in the process. This same problem could arise if your excited puppy and child grab for a ball or Frisbee on the ground at the same time. Supervision is critical when children and dogs are together. When structured and taught correctly, it can be a very fun, interactive game for both child and puppy.

No "Chasing the Puppy" Games

We highly discourage chase games. Children love to play chase the puppy games, but these games tend to develop into serious problems later in life. Please refer back to Chapter 5 for detailed information on chase games.

Do Not Play Keep Away—Teasing Is Not Fun

While keep away can be a fun game, it can also be a frustrating game to the puppy if he is never given an

Rules of play must be taught early on. This situation can quickly get out of control.

opportunity to obtain the object. When we teach a retrieve, we initially tease the puppy with an object and attempt to keep it away from him, hoping that the pup will think the toy is valuable, thus eliciting a greater interest in the object. The more interested the puppy is in the object, the more aroused he becomes, and the more he wants the toy. Once again, we are adults and trainers. We know exactly when to toss the toy before the pup gets frustrated or too aroused and leaps up and grabs at the toy, our arms, hands, or coat sleeve, to get the valuable object. Children do not.

We highly discourage chase games.

CASE STUDY
The Dog Who Loved Tennis Balls

A lovely family came to visit a few years ago. Their 3-year-old Golden Retriever, Duke, bit their son's 13-year-old friend's hand when he was outside tossing tennis balls to the dog. They were shocked since the dog loves this little boy. The family of the child that was bitten wanted them to put the dog down, or they would never permit their son to visit again. What a mess! After speaking to the son, he told Pia that the boy was teasing Duke with the ball. "Duke loves to be teased," he said. Duke was leaping from side to side trying to get the ball from the boy, getting more and more aroused, leaping up and grabbing at the ball in the boy's hand. The boy decided to throw the ball and, as he was tossing it, Duke leapt into the air for the ball. Instead of making contact with the ball, he bit down on the boy's hand.

Was this an accident as a result of a dog who was being teased, who never learned self-control and was pushed to the point of being overly aroused, where he could not control himself? Or, was this dog possessive of toys and a threat to children? Pia's final determination, after working with and testing Duke, was that he had never learned impulse control; had an obsession with tennis balls that turned into a compulsive behavior (he walked around with balls in his mouth all of his waking hours); and exhibited no guarding behaviors, since you could easily take the ball from his mouth, and he would easily give it up. He was gentle and kind in all respects, and Pia felt he should not be euthanized—he needed to be trained. After two sessions, Duke learned to sit and wait before balls were thrown, return with a ball in his mouth, and sit and drop the ball and wait for the next toss. Unfortunately, the boy's friend never came over again. Oh, by the way, Pia did tell the grandparents to stop bringing tennis balls over— they were tennis pros and Duke had 300 tennis balls in the yard!

No Roughhousing, Wrestling, or Tackling

As mentioned in Chapter 9, children should not be permitted to roughhouse, use force, strike, kick, or treat the puppy in any manner that can hurt or cause the puppy to become frightened or defensive. Out-of-control play must be avoided at all costs. If the children break the rules, then the children should get a time-out. The puppy should not be the one who is removed while the children continue playing. Too many parents remove the puppy from the scene when the children were the ones at fault.

Sending a child and puppy outside to play together unsupervised can be an accident waiting to happen.

When To Interrupt Play

There may be times when you need to interrupt the play session. Here are a few key behaviors to look for.

- The puppy is excessively mouthing, jumping, grabbing, and nipping at the child. This is a sign of a highly aroused puppy.
- Excessive barking means the puppy is becoming overly excited. The play could escalate into the behaviors listed above.
- No interruptions or pauses in play; the pup seems to have extra energy and is not tiring.
- One or both players are not having a good time.
- One or both players are feeling threatened and becoming frightened.
- One or both players are stalking the other or holding them hostage.
- The puppy begins to sniff the ground or attempts to get away by doing something else. This is a sign that the pup has had enough and is attempting to diffuse the situation.

- The puppy is becoming protective over a toy or other object and is becoming irritated at the child whenever the child attempts to take it away.
- The puppy will not give up the object and continually takes it to a safe area.
- The puppy is running away from the children in a frantic manner or looking for a safe place to hide.

We know this seems like a whole lot of rules and restrictions, but in reality a lot of it is just common sense. Because of it, our homes are very peaceable kingdoms, where dogs can be dogs and kids can be safe, and we are all thankful for it.

Types of Play To Encourage

Games for Children and Their Puppies

When games are played with puppies, it helps promote cooperation, control, and fun. At an early age, your puppy needs to learn that children are fun to be around and can be trusted. A good family dog is a dog who enjoys the company of children. Now is the time to begin teaching the puppy to enjoy your children. All of this can be done through games to foster the bond that the children and puppy will develop with time.

Find It

This game is quite handy when you can't find something, and is quite stimulating for the puppy, since he is using one of his senses to locate something that is hidden. Not only can this be mentally stimulating, but physically stimulating as well. Start off by getting three to four plastic cups or rubber containers. Turn the cups upside down on the floor and hide a treat under one cup. As the puppy begins sniffing, say, "Find it." The puppy should search out the treat and try to tip the cup

Teach your puppy to enjoy your children.

over to get it. If the puppy isn't sniffing around, then you may need to start off by using something that smells better or stronger, or put the treat partially under the cup so the puppy can see it. Gradually add more cups. Your children can wow their friends by playing the shell game—hiding the treat under one cup and moving the cups around—amazingly, the puppy knows (by using his sense of smell) which cup it's under. Eventually, once the pup understands the phrase, you can hide treats under different objects. As you progress, have one person hold the puppy in one room while the child hides the treat in another room. The child can then say, "Find it" and the puppy should search for the treat. Make sure the pup got a good sniff before hiding it, so he knows what he is looking for. Be careful not to walk toward the treat or stand next to it. The pup will be marking your scent, not finding the treat. If your puppy knows what his toys are called (i.e., Frisbee, ball) you can hide these objects and tell the puppy to "Find your Frisbee." You can teach your puppy the name of just about any object. Think how wonderful it will be if the puppy finds your keys in the morning!

Hide 'n Seek

Each time the puppy sees the child, say the child's name. Once the puppy is getting an idea that the name "Ryan" is associated with a certain child, hold the puppy and have Ryan run away and hide. Then say, "Find Ryan." The first hiding spot should be obvious so the pup can easily find Ryan and feel success. At first, Ryan may need to make some kind of noise to attract the puppy to him. Try to avoid saying anything else since this will simply confuse the puppy (too many words bring about confusion). As soon as the pup finds Ryan, Ryan should have a treat or toy ready to give to the pup for his accomplishment. If the pup knows your name, Ryan can then hold the pup and say, "Find Bobby," and the same scenario can begin. As the puppy gets better at the game, the children should make the hiding spots more difficult. This game can be done indoors and outdoors. The pup should always get some kind of a reward for a job well done.

Tug

We like to teach this game to children since it is a wonderful control game and teaches the puppy to relinquish objects when told. Yet, both parties *must* follow the rules of this game or the arousal level will get too high and the pup may start biting at clothing, hands, and more. This game will *not* cause your dog to become aggressive, as long as you teach self-control and rules. The puppy must first learn the rules from you, the adults, and be perfect at it before the children begin playing the game. You may find that some children or dogs have a difficult time following the rules. In this case, we do not recommend that you permit this game to be played.

- **Rule #1: Teaching "Take it."** The puppy must never take the tug object until you cue him to do so by saying, "Take it" or "Get it." Having it in your hands is not an invitation to jump up and grab for it. The larger and longer the tug object the better. We always start with a 3- to 4-foot fleece snake or other long object so the pup has plenty of toy to place his mouth on. Begin by teasing the pup with the object, shaking it on the floor or moving it around so he can't get it. Once the pup is excited about the toy and grabbing hold of it, you can then add the verbal cue. Be careful that the puppy is not grabbing the toy close to your hand.

- **Rule #2: Teaching "Give."** The puppy must relinquish the object when you say, "Give" or "Release." (We prefer not to use the phrase "Drop it" since people tend to yell this phrase, or say it with clenched teeth when the pup isn't dropping an item. Now we have both owner and dog with locked jaws.) Once the toy is in the puppy's mouth, you can show the puppy a toy of greater or equal value and, as soon as he opens his jaws to take the new toy, say, "Give" or "Release" and give him the other toy as a reward. If the pup isn't interested in the other toy, then you may use a food treat instead. As the pup is holding onto the toy, show the treat. As the pup is opening his jaw, add the cue, "Give" and give the pup the treat. Then you may tell him to "Take it" again. Some pups lose interest in the toy if you have treats on you. You may want to put the treats away or hide them. Keep playing until the pup realizes that you are not going to give him the treat until he takes the toy and gives it up when asked. Eventually, stop showing the treat or toy and tell the dog to "Give." If he does, tell

The puppy's mouth and child's hand are too close together during this tug game.

him to "Take it" again and the tug game is now the reward for giving it up. Use this cue for other objects but *never* yell or scream "Give!" or "Release!"—always remain calm.

- **Rule #3: No Accidental Misses**. If the pup is getting too aroused and grabbing at anything and everything (arms, hands, clothing) and not the toy, the game is over.

This is not a tug-*of-war* game, it is a tug game. In the wild, wolves or feral dogs do not war over objects if they are tugging on something. Typically, they are attempting to break a meal into pieces so both can eat. It is usually noncombative. Watch a litter of puppies tug with a toy. They both enjoy the game. They are not fighting over the object. Tugging typically is not part of fighting behavior. If they want the object that badly, they will stand their ground and guard it.

Follow the leader can be a great game for both puppies and children.

Follow the Leader

This is a great game that puts the child in charge as the leader. You can set up all sorts of obstacles using bars, tunnels, chairs, boxes, or natural objects such as trees, bushes, rocks, brooks, and more. Initially, the child may need to carry treats to encourage the puppy to follow him through, over, or under the obstacles. For those who live in the country, a favorite is rock jumping in a babbling brook. Not only does this teach the puppy to enjoy water, but both puppy and child get to have fun.

Fetch

Retrieving can be a wonderful interactive game, as well as give your puppy lots of exercise. The nice part of this is your child does not have to run around and be active at the same time. Unless the puppy is a natural retriever, this is not an easy behavior to teach a dog and takes time. Therefore, you must have patience. It may take several months before the puppy understands the concept of running to the object, picking it up, bringing it back, and releasing it. Some dogs play the game two or three times and stop or lose interest. If that's the case, then you may be moving too quickly or expecting too much. Stop after two sessions when the puppy still wants to play.

To start, adults should teach the game, then involve the child later. Find out what interests your puppy—balls, Frisbees (things that fly), things that squeak, or objects to tug on. Items for fetch should not be chew toys. After you choose your item, play

When a child and dog learn the rules of play, they can build a lifelong bond of friendship.

keep away from your puppy and, as he shows signs of wanting the toy, hold it out and say, "Take it" or "Get it." When the pup takes hold of it, say, "Yes!" and let it go. Right now, don't worry about the puppy relinquishing it. You will work on this separately. Once the pup understands what "Take it" means, move the object around on the floor so the pup can't get it and periodically say, "Take it." Always say, "Yes!" in a happy voice so the pup understands grabbing for the toy is right. Gradually move the toy around and have it roll on the floor as you say, "Take it." Don't expect the pup to automatically bring the toy back at this stage. Roll the object farther and farther away from you until the puppy is enjoying chasing after it and picking it up. Say, "Take it" just before the pup puts it into his mouth.

At this time, you can try clapping your hands, running backwards, patting the floor, or other moves to encourage the pup to return to you. He may drop it along the way, but don't worry. Run and pick it up and run

Establishing rules can avoid potential injuries. Here, proper behavior is exhibited by both child and dog.

away with it, then try again. If the pup brings it all the way back, lavish him with praise and even a few treats. Some pups may become distracted by food, so this may not be a good idea for those puppies. You might have another object that the pup really likes as an exchange. Now you can incorporate a release word. When the pup brings the object back, show him that you have something else that he wants, and as soon as he opens his mouth, say, "Give." Then start the game again.

You must play this game in various environments so the pup learns that he can fetch things inside and outside, not just in your living room. When outdoors, don't be surprised if your pup loses interest in the beginning, but once he gets hooked he'll love it!

Soccer

If you'd like to teach your pup to play soccer, our recommendation is to get a soccer ball that will not deflate easily if punctured by the puppy's teeth. People tend to get small toys for puppies, but the larger the better for this game, since the pup will have a more difficult time putting his mouth on it. Start off by gently kicking the ball around to encourage the puppy to chase after it. Your goal is that the pup starts to push it around with his nose or bats it with his paws. Give him a ton of praise when he is working the ball. Once he is catching on, you can set up goal posts. Again, this game can get out of control if the enthusiasm of one or the other becomes too much. Therefore, you need to set up rules. For example, kicking the ball into the goal post is not permitted. The ball must always be on the ground and roll in. This will eliminate the child accidentally kicking the ball and hitting the puppy in the face. If the child can't abide by this rule, then we discourage teaching this game. A puppy rule might be to stay focused on the ball and keep his mouth off shoes and pants.

Some games can get out of control if you don't establish rules.

Keep Away

Like tug, this can be a fun game, but can get out of control if you don't establish rules. This is a wonderful game to entice your puppy to play with certain toys. For example, take a ball and toss it back and forth between you and someone else. As soon as the puppy becomes interested and attempts to get the ball, don't toss it quite so high, so your puppy *can* get the ball. Everyone should cheer and praise the puppy. This is best taught after your puppy has learned a release word, like "Give" or "Release." One he has the ball, tell the pup to "Give" and start the game over again. Also, you can make this game more active by really keeping the ball from him—take a few steps side to side before tossing the ball. If the puppy gets too aroused, tell him to sit and reward him with the toy. It's important that the pup learn that he can get excited, but when you tell him to turn off he should obey. It's worth his while since he'll be rewarded for it.

Tricks for Children and Their Puppies

Below are a few tricks that can be taught to your puppy—they make for great entertainment when company is over. The key to teaching these tricks is that the cue word should *never* be said until the puppy is offering the behavior. The pup should be quickly and easily offering you the behavior several times before you add the verbal cue. Say the cue just prior to getting the behavior.

A fun trick to teach your dog is "Give me five."

Shake

This is a difficult behavior to teach, but can easily be put on cue when the puppy does it naturally. For example, after you give your pup a bath or anytime when he is wet, he will shake to get rid of excess water. When he is *about to shake*, say, "Shake" and praise him. If you do this often enough, not only will it make a fun trick, but this comes in handy for getting your dog to shake in the tub, rather than outside of it.

Paw or Give Me Five

Start off with your puppy sitting. Take a treat and hold it in front of your puppy's face. Move it up and off to the side to throw your puppy off balance. As soon as the pup lifts a paw, tell the puppy, "Yes!" and give him the treat. Gradually wait to give the treat until the puppy lifts his paw higher and higher. Another method is to place something in your hand and hold it in front of your puppy. Wait for your puppy to paw at your hand, say, "Yes!" and give him the treat. Gradually progress by putting the treat in a hidden place (behind your back) present your hand, and as soon as the puppy paws your hand give the treat from the hidden place. Eventually, you can open your palm and ask for "Paw" or "Give me five."

Bow

Not only is this a fun trick, it helps your puppy stretch, and can also help him elicit play in another dog. You can either put it on cue, or teach it. To put

it on cue, wait for the puppy to
stretch (typically every morning
just after waking) and say, "Bow"
each and every time he stretches.
To teach it, start with your puppy
standing. Hold a food treat in your
hand in front of your dog's face at
his nose. Lower the treat to the
floor in a diagonal line from his nose
slightly backward between his
front legs toward his tail. Your hand
should be on the floor and slightly

This is an example of a play bow.

under the puppy's chest. Most pups will lean backwards, arch their backs
and place their front elbows on the floor. As soon as the elbows are on the
floor (and before the rear hits the floor) say, "Yes!" and give him the treat.
If your pup doesn't do a full bow in the beginning, have patience. Take what
you can get and reward efforts until you have the full behavior. Eventually
get rid of the food treat and make the same hand motion with your hand as
you say, "Bow."

Spin

"Spin" is teaching your puppy to move in place in a tight circle. Your pup
might spin in one direction more easily than the other, since most dogs are
weaker and have less flexibility on one side (like people). Work on the
tighter side more often to help balance your puppy. Start with
your puppy standing. Hold a food treat in front of
your puppy's nose. Move the treat in a clockwise or
counterclockwise direction. As your puppy
follows it, say nothing until he has completely
spun around in a full circle. Then tell him, "Yes!"
and give him the treat. If he easily and readily
follows the food lure, then say, "Spin" just before

**There are
many tricks that
can be taught to
your puppy.**

Your curious puppy will enjoy exploring new places and learning new games.

you lure. As with other tricks, eventually get rid of the food in your hand and signal him to do it with your hand. If your pup should get stuck, reward the effort and keep trying to build to a full circle.

Crawl

This requires the use of different muscle groups. If you plan on teaching the follow–the-leader game, this exercise will help condition your puppy to use these muscle groups. Begin with your puppy lying down in a prone or sphinx position. Hold a food treat directly in front of the puppy's nose. Slowly move it slightly forward along the floor. As soon as your puppy starts to make a small effort to move forward while remaining down, tell him, "Yes!" and reward him with the treat. If the puppy should get up, start again. Gradually pull the food treat farther away until the pup has to move a little more. You can also use a prop (cocktail table or low chair) for your puppy to crawl under. This can come in handy if you have to get something under the sofa and can't reach it, but your puppy can. You can combine "Crawl" and "Get it."

After a fun day of learning tricks, remember to let your puppy rest.

There are many tricks that can be taught to your puppy. See our recommended reading list at the back of this book for more information on tricks and games.

Our hope is that your child and your puppy will learn to play together, resulting in an increased bond between the two. Children must be brought up learning to treat dogs with respect, and family dogs must be brought up with proper manners, so everyone in the family can benefit from having a canine best friend.

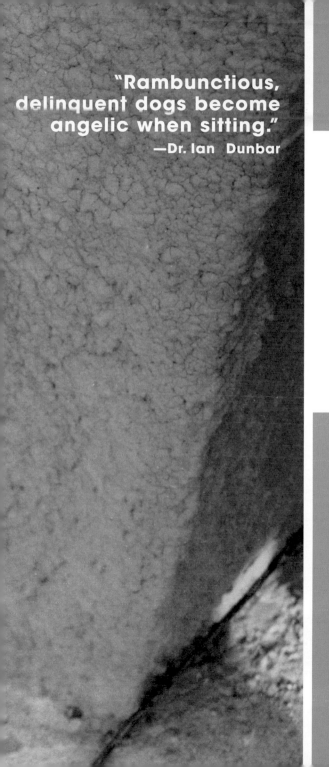

"Rambunctious, delinquent dogs become angelic when sitting."
—Dr. Ian Dunbar

Section 4

Your Puppy Becomes a Teenager

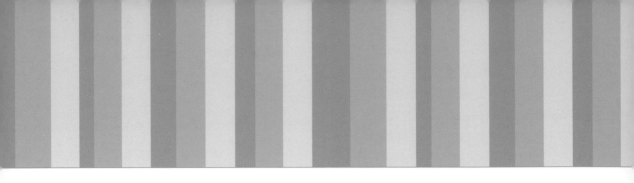

Chapter 11

The Juvenile Stage:
How to Cope and Survive

Puppies are dependent upon their mothers for food, shelter, and protection, just as children are with their parents. Both will vocalize when they are hungry, cold, lost, or feel threatened. The vocalization for food, warmth, and protection seems to lessen with age as both puppies and children become less dependent upon their parents, and the need to be taken care of decreases. They appear to have an air of confidence that wasn't present when they were young.

The Juvenile Stage (84 days through sexual and behavioral maturity) is commonly known as the adolescent period, or as we like to call it "the teenage years." The onset of sexual maturity can occur as early as 6 months of age, but behavioral maturity sometimes doesn't occur until the dog is a year or two old. Adolescence is a time of transition, with physical, mental, and emotional changes. Your dog is no longer fragile and needy, and his behavior patterns are going to be variable. He may respond to your cues and requests one day, and act as though he didn't hear them the next. He will exhibit puppy-like behavior, followed by the actions of a mature dog. Your children must now learn as well that the puppy is changing. The dog may greet your children with typical puppy exuberance one day, and ignore them the next. They need to understand that the dog is no longer a puppy. All of this will be frustrating to you, and even more so for the children.

A tired puppy is a good puppy. Exercise is very important!

The adolescent dog can be quite challenging. Although this stage will eventually pass, if you do not maintain good leadership, set rules, limits, boundaries, and structure in the dog's life now, the dog will become unmanageable. Many adolescent dogs end up in shelters because they exhibit unacceptable behaviors. Avoiding miscommunication during this stage will help keep the dog from ending up in a shelter, looking for a new home.

Adolescent Behaviors

The following are some behaviors that the adolescent dog will most likely exhibit. Like children, each dog will be different. Some go through a very mild transition, while others seem to be completely out of control. This is *not* a time to involve children in the discipline of the dog.

The adolescent dog can be quite challenging.

Increased Independence

Adolescent dogs appear to be more curious about the world and wander off to investigate. Checking back with you may no longer be part of their repertoire, since they feel they can now take on the world single-handedly. The need for security they once had as pups is beginning to leave.

KEEP IN MIND
Adolescent Exuberance

One sunny morning, Pia began to gather up some treats, balls, and Frisbees; the dogs were gleaming with joy in anticipation of what they expected to be a good morning for them. She and her dogs ventured out into the forest, walking alongside a partially frozen brook.

Her 6-year-old dog was by her side, her 8-month-old dog was, well where exactly was she? She had always stuck nearby Pia up until this morning. Pia turned to see that glorious little girl leaping over logs, crashing through broken ice in the brook, jumping into snow mounds, and blasting her way through thickets, with little or no care that she cut her tongue. She managed to run up and down the mountain four times by the time Pia got to the top. Pia looked at her 6-year-old as if to say, "Oh boy, here we go!" Like a child, take the adolescent dog on a new adventure and he is beside himself with joy.

You may feel like your dog is exhibiting the characteristics of a rebellious teenager. You may not be very important to the dog for a while, so making the dog work for the freedom that you give him is critical. In other words, you wouldn't give your 16-year-old the car keys to your new Mercedes as soon as he gets his permit to drive. Think of the adolescent dog as having a permit. You hold the license to drive, and you make the decision when it's time to go solo. (It should not be for many years!)

Increased Energy and Activity

Not only does the adolescent dog wander farther away, his energy level seems to be never ending. Adolescent dogs *do* require more exercise, since naptime is a thing of the past—there are far too many things to do and places to explore. Just like children, infants might nap several times a day, while you're lucky if you can get one nap per day with a toddler. Once they begin school, most children no longer need naps. In order to maintain control (and sanity), you will probably need to increase your dog's exercise routine. Dogs typically have activity highs in the morning and early evening. Most people think that a walk twice a day will suffice; it will not. Perhaps for an older dog, but not for your teenager. Dogs need to run and get rid of energy; dogs need to learn to keep their brains stimulated. The combination will tire your dog out.

Many people begin to give their dog more freedom in the house at this stage, thinking that the dog is housetrained and therefore safe. While he might be housetrained, you might see an increase in chewing. Chewing is a great stress reliever and helps release energy, especially for dogs who do not get enough exercise. As we discussed, earlier, a tired puppy is a good puppy; a tired teenager is even better. We have found that the majority of people who complain about their dog's behaviors admit that they do not give the dog adequate exercise. If you can't or do not have the time to exercise your dog yourself, then we recommend hiring a professional pet sitter or neighbor to see that your dog is getting the necessary amount of exercise. How do you know when enough is enough? If your dog can rest and remain calm in the house, does not chew on everything in sight, and his behavior is generally not over the top (unruly or out of control), then he has been well exercised.

Arousal Levels During Greetings and Play

Hopefully, you have diligently trained your puppy (and children) to understand what your rules are when there is any type of social interaction between the puppy and people. Make sure you do not lower your standards during this turbulent period. Your focus must be on encouraging your active youth to work for what he wants in life. His play styles may change from excitement to over-the-top arousal. Grabbing at clothing can turn into tearing clothing. Jumping up can turn into knocking people over. Barking might be self-reinforcing. Therefore, you must teach your dog to have a default behavior when he is aroused.

You must teach your dog to have a default behavior when he is aroused.

We teach "lie down" and "calm down" as a default behavior. This can be easily done by using a food lure. Begin with your dog facing you in a standing position. Place a treat between your thumb and forefinger and hold it in front of the dog's nose with your palm facing the floor. Slowly bring the treat down to the floor in a vertical direction toward your dog's front paws. Your dog should follow the food treat. Slowly move your hand along the floor between your dog's front paws toward his chest/belly, causing him to fold back and drop to the floor. Once your dog's elbows and rear are on the ground, tell the dog, "Yes," and give him the treat. Continue to do this until your dog easily and readily lies down following the food lure. Once he is consistently offering you the behavior, add the verbal cue "Down" or "Settle." You can progress to using the same verbal cue and hand lure *without* a treat to help the dog lie down. Once your dog is down, tell him, "Yes" and give a reward from a hidden place (from behind your back or from your pocket, for example).

Remember, it's not up to the dog to decide when enough is enough, it's up to you. Dogs *can* learn to listen to you during arousal periods. It may take a little more time, but they can do it. If you would not tolerate the behaviors the dog is exhibiting from your children, then do *not* tolerate them from your dog. For example, your dog may suddenly greet people with an overabundance of enthusiasm, exhibiting much more arousal than before. You wouldn't permit your teenager to exhibit poor manners simply because he is older. Saying please, thank you, and may I should still be part of your teen's vocabulary, and it should be part of your dog's as well.

Aggressive Actions

The most serious and concerning behaviors that can surface during the juvenile stage are threatening or aggressive actions. Examples of threatening or aggressive behaviors might be curling of the dog's upper lip, snarling, bared teeth, air snapping (the dog gives a quick snap toward a person but doesn't make contact), growling, or biting. These behaviors may occur when you or your children attempt to remove something from the dog's mouth, move him while resting, reprimand him, go near the food bowl, attempt to groom, etc. If your dog is exhibiting any of these behaviors, please make sure you contact a professional in the field right away before the situation gets worse. These behaviors *do not* go away with age, and can result in serious injury if not dealt with immediately.

What Is a Behavior Problem?

Before discussing some specific behavior problems that you might find in your adolescent dog, it is useful to understand canine behavior and behavior problems in general. Basically, canine behavior is anything that the dog does. It is only seen as a problem if you feel the dog is not in line with your expectations, beliefs, and what society expects of dogs. For example, while aggression is not an acceptable behavior in pet dogs, it *is* a normal canine behavior. What is acceptable varies from family to family. If we were to ask ten different people if they felt that the dog sleeping in bed with their child is a problem, we would probably end up with ten different viewpoints. What one person finds acceptable (or something they can live with), another may find totally unacceptable. Many people live with dogs who bite them; others would give up the dog after the first bite; yet another might give up a dog for growling. Some people live with dogs who soil in the house, thinking the dog can't be trained, while others would never tolerate this behavior.

Biting and soiling are both normal behaviors exhibited by dogs. For example:

- The dog has probably made many attempts to communicate that he is getting close to biting your child for picking him up every time he settles down for a nap. He may have communicated this by moving to a new spot whenever the child approached him.
- The dog who soiled the house probably communicated that he needed

to go outside to relieve himself on more than one occasion, but no one was present when he sat at the back door whining to be let out.

Getting Everyone on the Same Page

The most difficult part of our job as professionals is dealing with families who have differences of opinion as to what behaviors are problems and

Teach your dog proper kitchen manners early on.

what behaviors are not. What one person may tolerate, the other finds completely intolerable. If there is no consensus among the people in the household, then how can we expect the dog to behave?

One of the most common disagreements that causes family tension is whether or not to permit the dog on furniture, especially in the bed. The wife might want the dog sleeping under the covers curled up in a little ball against her back, while the husband wants the dog off the bed, since the dog growls at him every time he moves. The wife may not see this as a problem. Emotions take over—she feels sorry for the dog if they force him off the bed after a year of sleeping with them, and the husband finds this to be a serious problem (rightfully so). If the dog wasn't growling at the husband, then this probably wouldn't be a behavior problem. Both family members need to enjoy the company of the dog in their bed for it to work.

How Behaviors Become Problems

Dogs do not suddenly misbehave when they get older. They may have been carrying out the same behaviors for many months or years (soiling, chewing, barking, digging, etc.), yet it wasn't seen as a problem to most people when

Permitting a puppy to jump on children may not appear to be dangerous; however, this nuisance behavior can be intimidating and frighten children.

the dog was a puppy. With an older dog, those same behaviors are considered to be a problem. The main reason why so many behaviors turn into problems is that well-meaning people intermittently reinforce them, and now the behaviors become a nuisance.

CASE STUDY

The Puppy with the Jumping Up Problem

A family's 10-pound puppy who jumped up to greet people was not seen as a problem, since the puppy was so adorable and small that this wasn't unpleasant. Many times the family and friends encouraged or welcomed the jumping up to greet. As the pup grew and became more vivacious by using his teeth with greater force, hanging on to clothing, and knocking small children over, the greeting turned into a problem. The cute behavior turned into an annoyance. The family decided that they would no longer permit the puppy to jump up, yet while their efforts were well meaning, not everyone was in compliance. Johnny, their 17-year-old son, still encouraged the jumping up every day after school, and guests who claimed not to mind would calmly push the dog off, politely and softly saying, "There, there, good boy, now that's enough, sit," none of which the puppy understands. Once Johnny began following the rules, they were on their way to solving their puppy's jumping up problem.

Most behavior problems can be modified through management and training. However, not all problems can be "cured." Intervening early on is critical, before the dog has had an opportunity to be reinforced for the behavior over and over again, thus conditioning a patterned behavior. For example, if your dog is still soiling in the house at 6 months of age, he has not been carefully watched and taken out each and every time he needed to relieve himself. Think about it from the dog's perspective—

Most problems can be modified through mangement and training.

relieving himself *is* the reinforcement. The only consistency in the behavior is the fact that the dog is relieving himself. Sometimes the dog relieves himself indoors, sometimes outdoors. If no one is there to tell the dog where to go when he is about to relieve himself, how will the dog know what you expect? Seeing your angry face several hours later doesn't teach the dog to relieve himself outdoors. If anything, you are to be mistrusted since you appear to be unpredictable. Sometimes you return home in a good mood and other times you return angry and upset. The dog does not understand why. The dog may eventually assume that you do not like the sight of stool or urine. That must be it!

What Motivates Your Dog?

When behaviors are intermittently reinforced, the behavior increases or strengthens over time. You are simply conditioning the dog to continue to try, since there could eventually be a reward in it for him. Why do people get hooked on playing slot machines at the casinos, yet they don't appear

It is your job to find out what motivates your dog.

to be addicted to putting quarters into soda machines? They are always hopeful about hitting a jackpot.

Motivation has much to do with whether or not your dog continues to perform or offer behaviors. Motivation is internal with external incentives. It is your job to find out what motivates your dog. Like people, dogs must be motivated to perform the behavior, or they think, "Why bother?" Motivation incites us to take action. What motivates one will not necessarily motivate another. None of our dogs is particularly food motivated—they would prefer to play instead. As a result, neither of us has had to work especially hard making sure our counters are clear of food, since to our dogs, food isn't worth the effort to counter surf. But put a ball or Frisbee on the counter and you can bet they'd be motivated to jump up to retrieve it. Since we know what motivates, we make sure the balls and Frisbees are always hidden when playtime is over.

Dogs who are food motivated will continually jump up onto kitchen counters if they sometimes get rewarded, and sometimes get nothing. Even if it takes many attempts, if you're not careful they will eventually hit a big jackpot (the marinated steak!!). Owners of counter-surfing food hounds must make sure counters are always cleared off so the dog never gets rewarded for the behavior.

Believing the Dog "Knows Better"

This is a common misconception. If the dog did, in fact, know better, then why isn't the dog relieving himself outdoors? Dogs do not get back at you or get even because they don't like being left alone. Dogs are not spiteful nor do they sit up at night figuring out ways to get into trouble. Dogs enjoy peace and harmony in their lives, just as much as we do. Watch your dog's tail the next time you praise him. What dog gets enjoyment from being yelled at? We haven't met one yet.

Getting Off to a Good Start

If you were to sit down at a PTA meeting and talk to parents about the rules, structure, limits, and boundaries they have placed on their children, not one profile would look the same. Ask the same questions to dog owners, and you'll get a similar amount of variety.

To help establish a long-lasting, trusting relationship, make sure you reward the behaviors you like, and teach your dog that acquiescing to your requests is a smart strategy. It is equally as important that you prevent annoying, unwanted behaviors from occurring. Get yourself off to a good start by developing a tactic and game plan with the whole family for this challenging phase of your dog's life.

Consistency and persistence will pay off during adolescence.

Consistency and Training: Learn to Earn

Adolescent dogs demand attention when *they* want it. But, when *you* attempt to get his attention, you realize your dog forgot to tell you a little secret—he decided to change his name but never told you! This is typical adolescent dog behavior. Consistency and persistence will pay off during this time. Many people take time off from training because it can be more difficult now, with the hope that it will be easier once the dog matures. We would not give our children permission to do whatever they want during their teenage years, and then return to school when they turn 21. You must be consistent and continue to train your dog. If you do not, you will find that you have double the problems, and you will be burdened with undoing the inappropriate behaviors that the dog has developed. During this time, focus on rewarding your dog for good behaviors and avoid feeding into attention-getting behaviors.

Now is the time to "train his brain." Training should be part of your dog's daily routine and enforced throughout the day. It should not put more pressure on you or become burdensome. Use what your dog perceives as highlights as real-life rewards for compliance. Nothing in life comes to us for free; it shouldn't for the dog either. Tell your dog to do something before you

You must maintain leadership throughout your dog's life.

feed him, before you pet him, or before you open the door to let him outside in the yard. This is not asking too much. You are simply teaching the dog to say, "May I?"

Help him see that the quickest way to get what he wants is to simply comply with your requests. If you do this on a consistent basis, the dog will begin to offer you these behaviors instead of you having to ask for them. If you tell the dog to sit each time his meals are prepared, eventually he will start to sit on his own during meal preparation, without being asked. By shifting some of the responsibility to the dog to choose to want to comply in order to earn a reward, you take all of the confrontation out of your interactions. When people tell us that they have no time to practice, we make sure they are not trying to develop formal training sessions. If they are, the end result will be a dog who responds only during those training sessions. Instead, the dog must learn to listen *all of the time* and *throughout the day*.

Maintaining Leadership

To preserve sanity during this tumultuous time, you must maintain the leadership role that you established when the puppy came home. Dogs are social animals and are relieved when you take the pressure of being in charge off them. However, your position is going to be challenged during the juvenile stage, causing you to lose patience or, for some, want to use force. Leadership is not established or maintained through force. Leading with force (either physically or mentally) does not lead to respect.

Recall the people in your life who you considered to have exemplary leadership qualities and skills. What were those qualities and skills? Were these people yelling, screaming, and running around micro-managing the people around them? Were they in everyone's face, nitpicking every move their subordinates made, always focusing on what was going wrong and putting blame on others? Doubtful! There was a presence about them that you could see when they walked into a room. You felt it. There was no need for them to prove anything. They were organized, had a plan of action, clearly communicated that plan, and coached and supported through the process. They helped you achieve success.

The dog must learn to listen all of the time and throughout the day.

People who attempt to lead by bullying, manipulating, or dominating are typically insecure about their position. Manipulation aims at control, not cooperation, and ultimately drives people (and dogs) away. Victims of manipulation typically feel resentment, distrust, and eventually exhibit defensive behaviors as a result. Manipulation, through intimidation or otherwise, does not produce meaningful relationships; you will, in the long run, not succeed in being a respected and trusted leader for your dog.

You must establish realistic goals for your dog so he is able and willing to commit to listening to you. If you become satisfied with a dog who simply complies rather than commits, then you will get the minimum standards of performance from the dog. Think of compliance as a step toward commitment. Be aware of what your dog can accomplish. Be honest with yourself for your dog's sake. How much training have you formally done with the dog? Have you practiced trying to get the dog to sit at the park as another dog walks by? Have you worked on getting the dog to lie down by your chair in the veterinarian's waiting room? Is the request that you are giving your dog fair? Does he know how to respond in that particular situation? Set realistic goals for you and your dog. Achieve those goals and then raise the bar higher.

You must establish realistic goals for your dog.

CASE STUDY

The Puppy Who Became the Leader

One of Lynn's clients was a neighborhood family with a 5-year-old child, Sarah, and a 1-year-old dog. They obtained the dog from a breeder at 8 weeks of age and raised the dog in their home. This was their first dog, and they wanted to make sure they were properly providing for the dog. They fenced in their yard, giving the dog everything she wanted. Unfortunately, they never established themselves as leaders in this dog's eyes. They had no experience raising a puppy or training a dog, and never took the dog to a training class. The dog basically did whatever she wanted. She told them when she wanted to be fed, barked and scratched at the door to be let out, jumped at the screen to be let back in, and much more. They decided to seek professional help when the dog started to growl at Sarah whenever she approached the dog while eating. This also progressed to the dog growling at the adults during mealtimes. They were very concerned because Sarah would often have friends over, and although the dog had not yet bitten anyone, they began to worry. When Lynn consulted with the family and evaluated the dog, there was no question that the dog was *not* in charge in that environment, nor did she want to be. The dog was able to eat her meal with Lynn standing next to her and was not at all distraught when Lynn picked up her bowl. No complaints from the dog. The dog was taught some simple obedience exercises and was very willing to perform. She was relaxed and comfortable now that the role of leader had been taken off her shoulders. She did not want the job, but since no one in the family had taken on the role, she decided to take control and fill the position. The adults in the family took the dog through a series of obedience training classes and received help on how to handle the dog at home. Once the adults established leadership, the dog was happier and more relaxed and the behavior problems started to disappear.

Unfortunately, there is information out there that misguides people into thinking they must demonstrate to their dogs that they are dominant over them or the dogs will never respect them. People are mistakenly encouraged to get submission from their dog by pinning him to the floor, rolling him over onto his back, and hard staring at the dog, waiting for him to avoid eye contact, based on the theory that a dog who makes eye contact with his owner does not respect him.

Children are not leaders, and should not be asked to be responsible for a dog's actions.

This thinking is antiquated, completely unnecessary, and has no scientific basis behind it. Leadership is *not* about dominance and submission. We have owned more than 15 dogs between us, all role models wherever we took them. Not one of these dogs obeyed because we used force or rolled them over into an alpha position. That's why we can have our dogs off-leash without fear of losing them. Followers don't run away from home; nor do they run away from their leaders (unless they don't trust or respect them). Followers work in harmony with their leaders, and find it a true honor to be with them.

Children Are Not Leaders

We continue to stress throughout this book that no child should ever be left alone with a dog, or be responsible for the dog's actions. Many dogs become victims of children since children do not have the cognitive ability to be able to set limits for dogs. They have enough trouble understanding limits themselves. Eventually, the dog is forced to hit a threshold that can be devastating to both child and dog.

CASE STUDY
The Dog Who Didn't Want To Stay Outside

A distraught mother called us, concerned that she might have to get rid of the family dog. The dog had always been good with the children, but recently began baring his teeth at them. Most recently, the dog growled when the children attempted to take the dog outside. After spending an hour with the mother and children, and extrapolating as much background information as possible, we concluded that there was too much responsibility put on these young children with no adult supervision. The children were in charge after school until the mother got home from work (a short half-hour). What could go wrong in this short period of time? A great deal.

The children were assigned to take the dog out to play, making sure he didn't get into trouble. These children and dog were never taught about rules of play. The children were tag teaming while playing competitive games with the dog, never realizing or understanding when the dog had enough. The dog made many attempts to communicate to them that he wanted to return to the house, but the children were told that the dog needed fresh air, and insisted that the dog participate much longer than he could tolerate. The dog made many attempts to avoid being chased, tackled, and grabbed. All of this was entertaining for the children, but *not* the dog.

When the mother returned from work, the dog was relieved and spent much of his time seeking her attention and protection. The dog started to growl at the children whenever they approached the mother. Mom felt the dog was protecting her when, in actuality, the dog was pleading to the children to leave him alone. Once we taught the children the proper rules of play and how to appropriately handle the dog, the dog was given a chance to regain trust in them, and the relationship and bond was reestablished.

Establishing Boundaries, Limits, Rules, and Structure

Domestic dogs are given far too many privileges without the establishment of boundaries, limits, rules, and structure. The latitude given to domestic dogs is far beyond what they can handle. The result, many times, is a one-sided relationship where the family is catering to whatever the dog wants according to the dog's terms. The relationship is, at times, dysfunctional and unhealthy, to say the least. No relationship can be sustained when it is one sided, whether a marriage, a child and parent, siblings, or a person and a dog.

Be Aware of Demanding Behaviors

The case described above is not out of the ordinary; however, most cases do not get to this extreme. To avoid even getting close, it is critical that you maintain awareness about what your role is in the relationship. Neither the adults nor the children should ever become the dog's personal servant. To help analyze if you are down the path for disaster, here are a few questions for you to answer.

- Does your dog tell you to let him out every 20 minutes by barking or scratching at the door?
- Does your dog then jump on the door or bark when it is time to come in?
- Does your dog tell you when his water or food bowls are low or empty?
- Does your dog tell you when it is time for him to eat?
- Does your dog bark or sit in front of the cookie jar waiting for you to deliver, simply because he wants one?
- Does your dog demand to play *only* on his terms, and when you are not paying attention to him (perhaps on the phone, at the computer, reading a book, or eating)?
- Does your dog stop playing when he has had enough?
- Does your dog bark at you when you are on the phone, or nudge you for petting when you are sitting down for a cup of tea?

- Does your dog push his way into the middle when you are interacting with the children?
- Does your dog tug at your sleeves or pants leg to get your attention?
- Does your dog push his way in front of you at the front door when the bell rings?

If you said yes to any of these questions, then your dog is doing a wonderful job training you. Inadvertently, you have been reinforcing his demanding behaviors. Before it's too late, begin to put your dog on a schedule for feeding, playing, walks, and rest time. Make sure you have met these needs for your dog, then you can and should ignore the dog's demands to be let out, to be fed, to be pet, played with, etc. *You* establish rules, not the dog. By all means, pet, play, and cuddle with your dog, but on your terms and when it is convenient for you. The result will be a dog that listens to *you*!

Managing the Environment

The environment can be quite interesting and rewarding to your dog (both indoors and out). It should not be given away freely. It is too valuable and even more critical now that you have an adolescent dog. Please refer back to Chapter 3 for more detailed information on setting up your dog's environment.

Car Problems

Permitting your dog to run free in the car is not only unadvisable but also dangerous. If he is barking at everything that goes by, or goes ballistic when a gas station attendant appears in the window, at the bank drive-through, toll gates, etc., your dog is controlling the environment. Furthermore, you are risking getting into an accident, since your attention is not on the road, but on the dog. There is no need for the dog to sit in your lap when you are driving. One fender bender going 15 miles per hour can throw your dog through the windshield.

Unwanted Behaviors in the Yard

Your dog should not behave like a hired guard when outside in the yard.

While there is absolutely nothing wrong with your dog barking a warning that a trespasser is coming, the barking should immediately cease when you, the leader, appear. The dog should look to you for guidance. Is this person someone we need to be concerned with or not?

Establishing rules and boundaries early on can lead to a healthy bond between child and dog.

Think about all the fun and trouble an adolescent dog can get into if left in the yard alone. Dogs dig. Why? So they can bury things, find your tulip bulbs, get the mole that was burrowing there last night, find cool earth to lounge in, or get rid of pent-up energy. Dig where? Your gardens and lawn, of course.

Dogs like to chase. Why? It's fun, especially if they have practice and get better at it and actually catch the prey. Do you have squirrels, chipmunks, deer, stray cats, or rabbits that wander through your property? Very exciting for your dog. Where do they chase? In the yard, across the street, or into the woods, if they can.

Dogs chew. Why? Because it feels good, and the act of chewing helps sore gums and gets rid of pent-up energy. What will they chew? Your patio furniture, shrubs, plants, decks, grass, rocks, or just about anything else they can find. (One Lab we know ate his doghouse and finished off with the owner's motorcycle—fiberglass, tires, and all.)

Dogs bark. Why? This is how they communicate, sound an alert, and more. When do they bark? When left outside alone, or just about anytime for any reason. They bark to come in, when someone or something passes by, at animals, etc. Think twice about giving your dog this freedom.

The key factor to remember when your puppy turns into an adolescent dog is to maintain control and have patience. If you're careless with your communication, your dog will be casual with his responsiveness to you. Set your standards high. If you become too lenient, your dog's behavior will rapidly slide. Make sure you are fair and do not ask your dog to do anything that he is not capable of doing. If you haven't formally taught him to come to you when distracted (like when he's chasing a squirrel in the yard), do not expect him to just because he is older. It is unfair and unkind to expect your dog to respond when it is truly beyond his ability. Do not abuse your authority. Use it wisely and kindly, and you will gain his boundless trust.

CASE STUDY
The Dog Who Controlled the House

A couple found themselves polarized as a result of the relationship they had gotten themselves into with their dog. Neither could agree as to what the dog should be, and how the dog should be treating the children (not how they treat the dog). They purchased a breed at 7 weeks of age that was supposed to be good with children. Any dog can be good with children if brought up correctly; any dog can be bad with children if brought up incorrectly (especially if there is no adult leader).

This dog slept in bed with the adults, but neither person could move once they were in bed, or the dog would bite them. The children could not enter the bedroom without the dog leaping off the bed and attacking them. To keep the children safe, the parents' bedroom was off limits to the children. At 5 a.m., the dog woke the couple up demanding to be let out and fed. The couple complied, thinking the dog needed to relieve himself. They attempted to ignore him a few times and the dog urinated on the bed (yes, while they were still there!). At 7 a.m., the dog began barking, demanding to go for his morning walk. If the owners attempted to leave the house without walking him, he would bite them on their departure. He spent hours sitting on the back of the sofa looking out the window and barking at passersby. When the children came home from school, the arousal level went up. If they invited friends over, the dog would hold them hostage in their bedrooms. As time went on, the parents decided that the children were not permitted to have friends over. The children eventually got tired of the dog and didn't want any part of him (understandably).

The goal was to try to help the owners regain control. It was important to make sure the family's emotional conflict about what their role and responsibility was did not revert back to feeling sorry for the dog. They felt guilt, anger, fear, sadness, and much more. At times, they blamed the dog for being selfish, spiteful, and vengeful. Then they would blame themselves for being poor dog parents. Their moods and emotions shifted daily, which only increased the dog's anxiety. When they were angry at the dog, they punished him (resulting in more bites). When they were angry with themselves, they invited the dog back into the bed.

How could things have gotten this bad? Because everything happened on the dog's terms. These problems certainly did not happen overnight. The dog was 2 years old, and the behaviors gradually got worse, since the adults had a difficult time establishing leadership. There were no boundaries set for this dog, the rules were made to be broken, and the dog never learned to say, "May I?" This dog was spoiled, and the adults catered to the dog. Unfortunately, this family could not continue to live with their dog despite their good efforts to rectify the problems.

Believe it or not, the children in this family were very well behaved. The adults' good parenting skills unfortunately did not carry over to the dog. If it had, they would probably still be living with the dog.

Chapter 12

Dogs and Their Resources: How To Avoid Problems

Now that you have a puppy, your house is probably filled with all sorts of dog toys, bones, and chews. Having two puppies crazy about toys and bones, we found ourselves experimenting with many different types of products to find which worked best for us. These items are a great source of fun and enjoyment for most dogs, and a necessity if you have a puppy, but you must make sure they are used properly. These seemingly innocent items often become a source of problems for many dog owners. For example, the puppy's things are probably scattered on the floor and intermingled with your children's toys. In a puppy's mind, what's on the floor is up for grabs. To say that a puppy can distinguish between his stuffed toy and your child's stuffed toy, his ball and your child's ball, or a rawhide and a pair of leather shoes is putting far too much pressure on this little playful animal. Your puppy will make a game out of everything and chew whatever is available to him. The pup knows nothing about "his" and "yours." We'll show you how to avoid these problems, so you can live in harmony with your canine friend.

Appropriate tug play between child and puppy.

Toys for Playing

There are many different types of toys on the market. Before heading out to the store, decide what types of games you would like to play with your puppy. Will you play tug, fetch, or soccer? Since these are interactive toys you will use when you want to play with your puppy, they should not be left on the floor for your puppy to pick up and chew. Most of these toys, if left unattended with your puppy, will be chewed in a matter of minutes. Not only is that costly for you, but it could also be very dangerous for your puppy. Both of our pups enjoy tearing apart stuffed animals, especially those that make noise. We were quite surprised by what was inside some of the toys given to us as puppy gifts—layers and tubes of plastic, metal pieces, small squeakers, and some even had small nuts and bolts. Therefore, be careful what you leave around the house—your pup might chew and shred the new toy, swallowing a squeaker inside. There are toys that are not safe for the pup to play with unsupervised.

You may decide to try playing tug games with your puppy (please refer to Chapter 10 on how to properly play tug). Tug can be a great way for children to interact with their puppy. A good tug toy should be a minimum of 3 feet long, and made of a sturdy material that won't easily break apart. You want your hand, or your child's, to be at one end of the toy and the puppy's mouth at the other, a safe distance away.

Toys that the puppy can fetch or at least chase after are also a lot of fun and easy to use for children old enough to throw them. Try using a Frisbee (there are a lot of dog Frisbees on the market), or a ball that can be easily thrown. Large sturdy balls, like soccer balls or big plastic balls, are great fun as well for playing outdoors. You and the children can kick the ball around and encourage the puppy to join in and push it with his nose.

Too Many Toys

If you don't want it chewed, don't leave it on the floor.

Many people rush out to purchase a considerably large number of toys as soon as they get their puppy. In fact, puppies can often end up with more toys than the children have. You wake up one morning and look at your living room floor and can't believe all the stuff that's there. Yet you are frustrated because your puppy keeps chewing the children's toys, your sneakers, and anything else he may find. You don't understand why this happens, since you've given him tons of his own toys to play with. Don't be too hard on your puppy. As mentioned, you must remember that he does not understand, especially during the early months, that he is not allowed to use everything he finds on the floor as his own personal chew toy. You must also think about this from the puppy's perspective. A great percentage of the toys or objects on the floor *are* his—how can he possibly tell what is and what is not his? To the puppy, it seems that all things on the floor are his. So, when you take your sneakers off in the middle of the toy field, it is not surprising that he would think nothing of picking them up. If you don't want it chewed, don't leave it on the floor.

Having both the kids' and puppy's toys all over the floor can also present other problems. The puppy and child could attempt to pick up the same toy at the same time. Your child may be giving child toys to your puppy, and your puppy may be dropping dog toys onto your child's lap. Or perhaps the child sees the puppy about to take one of his or her own toys and quickly runs over to try to get it first. Depending on the puppy's personality, he could respond in many ways. The pup might:

- Quickly grab at the toy with his mouth and end up grabbing your child's hand that got in the way.
- Feel the need to protect and guard this object to prevent it from being stolen from him by the child.

- See the child coming and run away with the toy in his mouth, leaving a screaming, crying child running after him.

These things will leave the child more frustrated and the puppy more annoyed. A young child might even end up hitting the puppy out of frustration and inability to cope with the situation; and the puppy could end up nipping or biting the child to make him or her go away. What started as a child and puppy playing peacefully on their own in the same room with their own toys, could end up in a confrontation in a matter of seconds. You do not want to ever place your child and puppy in that situation, so *supervise*.

Toy Box

We recommend getting a toy box for all your puppy's toys. This can be as simple as a low-sided cardboard box (for those pups who aren't active chewers) or a heavy plastic storage tub. Put all of your puppy's toys in this box and show him where it will be kept. The sides must be low enough that your puppy can get his head over the side to reach in and take a toy out of the box. You can drop in a few treats or stuff a few chew toys with treats at the bottom of the box, which will encourage your puppy to put his head in there. Allow the puppy to take a toy out of the box and bring it into the room with the family. Each and every time the pup goes to the toy box, lavish him with praise, or interact with him. The pup must learn that taking things from *this* box is rewarding. When he is no longer playing with the toy, put it back in the box. You want him to learn that his things are found in that box, not lying all over the floor. If he takes something from the floor that is not his, calmly take it from him and bring him over to his toy box.

Toys and Bones for Chewing

One of the more frustrating puppy behaviors for most people is the puppy's strong need to chew. Anything, everything, everywhere! You must remember that the act of chewing is very natural and necessary for puppies (and older dogs). Dogs chew for a number of reasons: to work the teeth and gums when teething, to help release pent-up energy, to relieve stress or boredom, or just because it's fun. If you are not supervising your puppy, and he is wandering around the house, he will find things to use for his chewing pleasure, and these things will not likely meet with your approval. Remember, if you cannot watch your puppy, then he should be in his crate. He is safe there, and your house and belongings will be safe from destruction.

The dog's toy box.

We have divided chews into two categories: chew toys, which are non-chewable objects designed for a puppy to chew on and play with; and chew bones, which are chewable items safe for chewing and ingestion.

Chew Toys

A good chew toy is ideally one that cannot be destroyed or consumed. For example, a fuzzy snake tug toy used for playing is not a chew toy. If the puppy chews on that toy, he will begin to break off pieces and possibly swallow them. It is easy to destroy and too dangerous to be a good chew toy. Some items that make great chew toys are sterilized bones (never "cooked" bones), heavy knotted ropes, and a variety of products that hold and/or dispense treats, made from heavy rubber and plastic materials. Stuffing the toy with treats helps the puppy to become interested in the item and want to chew on and play with it. Look for items that are listed as indestructible in your pet store. There is at least a better chance that your puppy will not chew pieces off it, although there is no guarantee. Try to find a few items that your puppy likes from the ones mentioned above. They are safer to leave with the puppy, and can be placed in his crate with him when you are leaving him alone for a few hours. An appropriate chew toy will not only help satisfy your puppy's need to chew, but it will give him a constructive and safe way to occupy his time.

Chew Bones

Appropriate chew toys will help satisfy your puppy's need to chew.

There are a number of good chew bones that are safe. We recommend natural products, such as bully sticks, lamb's ears, and raw butcher bones. The puppy can gnaw on them, many of which will soften and gradually wear away. The puppy should be supervised at all times when given this type of chew item. You want to be sure that the puppy cannot or does not break off a big piece and swallow it whole. Many dogs have been known to chew off large, flat pieces of rawhide bone. They can easily lodge in the throat when the dog attempts to swallow, causing the dog to choke and not be able to breathe. If you are not present, a puppy could choke to death.

Try different items on your puppy to see which type he prefers and to get a feel for what his chewing style is like. Some dogs chew with gusto and will completely devour one of the chewable items mentioned above in a matter of minutes. Others are more casual chewers, and a chewable item could last for a couple days or weeks. We do not recommend leaving your puppy alone with one of these items, just in case he has difficulty while chewing or swallowing it. Better safe than sorry. Leave him with a safe item from the chew toy list, instead.

Please remember that adult dogs like and need to chew as well. This is not a behavior that goes away with time, although many adult dogs' chewing needs are far less intense than when they were puppies.

If You Catch Your Puppy in the Act

If, at any time, you observe your puppy chewing on something inappropriate (like your sneakers, coffee table leg, or baseboard molding), immediately interrupt him by making a noise (like clapping—no yelling), then calmly go to him and interrupt the chewing. Redirect him to something that is appropriate to chew (one of his chew toys or bones). You should then praise him for chewing on the acceptable item. Never shout at your puppy from a distance or go running quickly toward him to try to stop him. If he was chewing on an item that he could pick up (like your sneaker), this could start the chase game. The chase may be so much fun that your puppy goes back to chewing the inappropriate item just to start up the chase game again.

Attempting to remove an object may result in a warning from the puppy that the child will not understand.

Guarding: "Hey, That's Mine!"

A puppy may find a chew toy or bone quite pleasing and valuable and not want to relinquish the item. As a result, he may guard it from whomever he thinks *might* take it away, or when a family member or stranger attempts to take it from him. With some dogs, this problem can be very serious. They might show their teeth, curl their lip, snarl, snap, or growl when someone is near them, including family members. This may even occur when a person simply walks by them when they are chewing on the item. It is critical, especially if you have children, that you not take this lightly. It will not go away with age. Try to prevent this situation from happening, but if it does happens you must take action immediately.

Prevention

Do not allow your children to try to take one of the puppy's chew toys or bones from his mouth. The puppy may view these as very valued possessions and may not be willing to let the child take them from him. We always encourage children to give things to the puppy and avoid taking things away.

If the puppy has something in his mouth that he should not have, or is potentially dangerous to him, the child should tell an adult, not take it upon himself to remove it.

You should first teach your puppy to relinquish objects that he has in his mouth (see Chapter 10 on how to teach "Give"). Once he knows this command, when you say, "Give" the puppy should drop whatever he has in his mouth. Practice this on items that the puppy does *not* highly value before trying it with his chew bones. It is important that you can take things from your puppy without a confrontation. He must respect that you, as the leader, may need to remove things from his mouth, and you are entitled to do it. It could one day save his life. Your puppy will not likely have the same respect for your children, and it can be dangerous for them to try. If you need to take something from the puppy, calmly walk up to him, say his name, and tell him "Give" as you take the chew item. Do not say it in a soft or questioning voice, but do not yell at him either. Use a very confident matter-of-fact voice. Your attitude should be "I am here, and I need to take your bone now." Once you have the chew item, you can give the puppy a really yummy treat for giving it up.

Early Warning Signs of a Potential Problem

Most pups give you subtle signs that there may be a guarding problem. It is important for you to recognize these warning signs rather than waiting until your puppy exhibits any more serious threatening or aggressive behaviors. You should talk to the breeder or rescue group about whether or not the puppy was tested for guarding behaviors. Could they remove items from the puppy's mouth with no problem? If not, what did they do when he refused to give it up?

- If your pup is always taking his chew toys and bones and hiding with them (e.g., under a piece of furniture, in his crate, taking it to another room), he is probably telling you that he wants to be left alone. When you give your puppy these items, he should happily take it to a comfortable area to chew it, and you should be able to remove it from him if necessary. While you don't want to constantly remove bones from the pup's mouth, you certainly need to make sure that you can. Encourage him to stay with you and chew the bone out in the open. Do *not* permit children to bother him at this time. The pup must learn to relax and not be concerned that the child will bother him every time he is chewing on a toy; if the child does, eventually the pup will get annoyed, hit a threshold, and tell the child to back off. Imagine every time you sat down to read a good book, someone in the family took it away from you? You might end up being a closet reader.

CASE STUDY
The Dog Who Didn't Want To Be Chased

A young couple came in with their 7-month-old infant and 1-year-old hound mix, Benny. He comfortably chewed on his chew bone while lying in the middle of the kitchen floor. However, now that the child was beginning to crawl, he was able to interact more with the dog. Benny was on the same level as the infant, and he had something that interested the child. Benny would give very good warning signs that he did not want the child bothering him when he had a chew bone. When the child crawled up to Benny, Benny would always get up and walk away. However, the parents thought it cute when the child crawled faster in an attempt to catch Benny. They said Benny didn't seem to mind and appeared to enjoy the game. Yes, Benny did mind—his warning sign was removing himself from the situation. (Good boy, Benny!) If the child were permitted to continue to chase after Benny, eventually the dog could become frustrated and perhaps bite. This is why seeking help early is critical to help resolve problems.

- If your puppy is always removing himself when the children are home, entering the room, or getting too close, this is another signal to you that he is uncomfortable when they are around. Remember the reading analogy? When you are reading that good book and you see your young toddler approaching, knowing that the child is going to take the book away, depending upon your mood, you might get up and walk away, stand your ground and tell the child, "No," or become upset and angry—your dog probably feels the same way.

- If your pup's chewing quickens every time someone approaches, this is a signal to you that the pup is trying to eat it as fast as possible before it is taken away.
- If your puppy suddenly freezes and stops chewing as someone approaches, then goes back to chewing after the person has gone past him, this is a signal that he is afraid someone might take the chew bone from him.

Problem Solving

The key behind avoiding guarding problems is to convince the pup that nothing in your house has value. Have you ever watched your children when they have gotten something new? They take it off to the side and don't want anyone near them, especially their siblings. They feel it has value and want to be left alone with their wonderful toy. Dogs can be the same way. Therefore, whenever your puppy has something, always remain calm, keep your voice as mellow as possible, and when you ask the pup to "Give" (regardless of what it is), reward him with something else. This doesn't have to be a lifelong exercise. You are simply establishing a pattern for good behavior. For example, if you tell the puppy to "Give" his bone, you might want to smear a little cheese onto it, and give it back to him. Now, giving the bone up certainly was worthwhile, since you made it even tastier.

If at any time you are concerned with the behavior of your dog, especially if he growls at you over a certain item, you should immediately stop giving those items to your dog and seek the advice of a professional in the field. You do not want to put yourself, your family members, or friends in a position to be bitten by your dog.

Taking Things from the Puppy

Not only will your puppy try stealing things that are not his, but your younger children will probably try to steal or take things from the puppy. Supervision is critical to avoid problems. Let's say your puppy picks up one of the children's toys and lies down to play with and chew on it. Your child sees the puppy with a favorite toy in his mouth. This angers or upsets the

A child attempting to remove something from a puppy's mouth could result in the child being bit.

child, who then tries to take back the toy. Young children will simply walk over to the puppy and grab the toy right from the puppy's mouth. The child might even attempt to give the puppy a reprimand, or even worse, spank the puppy for "being bad." Depending on the temperament of the puppy and how much he is enjoying that toy, the child may end up the victim of a dog bite. Most likely the puppy will warn the child not to try to remove the toy by freezing, staring, or even growling, but the child is not going to understand those signals, and will continue to go for the toy. Everything escalates, since the puppy's warnings did not work. While some puppies will run away to avoid having the toy taken from them, some might choose to stand their ground and fight for this new possession.

Don't automatically think that the puppy is having fun when he is being chased. If the puppy feels the object has value and runs off, this is one time when he does *not* want to be chased. He may run to a hiding spot, like under the coffee table or behind the sofa. If the child reaches in to grab for the object, the pup might take action—and it's not going to be an action you will like. Once again, if you are

Supervision is critical to avoid problems.

Teach giving....not taking.

experiencing any of these problems with your puppy, please consult a professional in the field.

Teach Giving Not Taking

Young toddler-age children are just starting to learn to share. They go through a stage where everything is "theirs." As a one-and-a-half-year old, Lynn's daughter would collect as many toys as possible and carry them around in her arms. They were hers, and she did not want anyone else to have them. She had to learn that it was a good thing to give her possessions to other people, that sharing was the polite way to play, and that it was not polite or acceptable to take or grab things from another child's hands. Of course, as luck would have it, Lynn had a young puppy in the house at the same time her daughter was going through this stage. Anything that the puppy had in his mouth, whether it was his or not, she would want to grab from him. If Lynn had let this go on, it could have been disastrous. The puppy could have ended up running away every time her daughter approached, for fear of losing the object he had; or, even worse, may have decided to stand his ground and protect the object. Neither of these would have been desirable.

Lynn had to constantly supervise to be sure she could interrupt her daughter's attempts to take something from the puppy. She taught both of her children that if the puppy had something that did not belong to him, they were to get her—not take it from him themselves. The next step was to teach her children to give the puppy his own toys, rather than always wanting to take things from him. You want your puppy to view the children approaching him as an asset, not a threat.

Food Guarding

Your puppy probably gets very excited over the sight of his meal being prepared and placed in his food bowl. After you place the bowl on the floor, he happily digs in. Most puppies love mealtime (although there are puppies and older dogs that are picky, finicky eaters). Puppies who have the opportunity to spend the early weeks of their lives with their mother and littermates are accustomed to eating with other puppies close by. When the puppies are being weaned from their mother and ready to eat more solid food, most breeders will put the meal for the litter in one big food dish, and all the puppies gather around to eat together. It is quite an enjoyable sight to see.

Puppies learn at a young age to eat with others close beside them. People should not fall into the trap of that old advice, "When the dog is eating, leave him alone." When they do follow that advice, the food bowl gets placed in a corner of the room, in a room separate from the rest of the family, or perhaps in his crate so the dog can eat in peace. Of course peace is always nice when eating (as opposed to running, screaming kids flying by him as he is trying to eat, stepping in his food bowl and tripping over him as they run by). But your puppy does not need to eat in isolation. There is nothing wrong with having the puppy eat in a high-traffic area, such as the kitchen, and we actually recommend it. A puppy who continually eats in isolation and gets used to it could become threatened by or fearful of the approach of a person or other dog while he is eating.

Depending on the puppy, he may display his feelings in different ways—some of the signs are obvious to most people and others are not. A dog may suddenly freeze while eating and become stiff with his head still in the food bowl. He may raise the hair on the top of the shoulder and back (hackles), curl his lip, growl, snarl, or stand over the bowl. Some dogs might eat faster and inhale the food, while others will show a whale eye, where you see the whites of the dog's eyes and the eyeball is in the corner of the eye. Most dog owners do not see or notice these warnings and changes in body language that their dogs are displaying—and young children will definitely not notice them. If a person continues to approach a dog who has given these warnings, the dog may feel the need to defend this valuable resource (his food), and may resort to lunging or snapping at you, or even biting.

Teach Your Puppy to Relax Around the Food Bowl

Many people, in trying to do the right thing to prevent food guarding from happening, will frequently take the food dish from the puppy while he is eating, just to show they can. This will not help to make the puppy more comfortable about having you near. He will start to become worried when you approach, since it often results in him losing his dish. This could even create the problem you are hoping to avoid.

Instead, get your puppy used to you being near his food bowl from very early on. Stand next to him and talk quietly to him. You can get a really yummy treat (like a piece of meat leftover from your dinner) and let him see that a hand that approaches his food dish puts really great stuff in his bowl, rather than taking it away. He will start to look forward to your approach while he is eating in anticipation of getting a treat.

You want to teach your puppy to relax and feel comfortable when people are standing or walking by right next to him while he is eating. Ideally, if children are involved, the puppy should get used to being touched while eating as well. Most children will walk by their dog while he is eating and pat him on the back on their way by. Watch the dog when this happens to see if there is any change in his eating (he may start to gobble his food down as fast as possible, or stop eating entirely). If so, move your children away for safety's sake and consult a professional behavior counselor.

CASE STUDY

The Puppy Who Wanted His Food Bowl

We recently met with the owners of a 6-month chocolate Labrador named Hershey. Hershey was wonderful with the four young children in the family. They told us that the children could "do anything to the dog," a phrase that always concerns us. (What *are* they doing to the dog, exactly?) Recently, Hershey started to growl at the youngest child, Kyle (age 7). He spent the most time with Hershey, playing with him, feeding him, taking him for walks, and Hershey even slept in his bed at night. The parents were shocked. Why would Hershey growl at his favorite? We found out that Kyle had been told to take Hershey's food bowl away to prove that he was in charge. When Hershey was a younger puppy, he didn't seem to mind. However, at 6 months of age, Hershey certainly was getting a bit tired of Kyle constantly bothering him during his mealtime.

If you are going to test to see if your puppy willingly relinquishes food or other items, there is no need to continue testing for months, and absolutely no reason to test every single time he has one of these objects. Poor Hershey simply got fed up. It wasn't that Hershey no longer liked Kyle, he was simply telling him to stop bothering him every time he was eating. And Kyle certainly didn't like it when Hershey bothered him while eating. But Kyle was not to blame—he was just doing what he was told. The only problem was no one told him when to stop. Children do not know when enough is enough.

Sleeping/Resting Areas

Puppies, like children, tire and need naps or quiet times. It's important to teach your children that when the puppy is sleeping or resting in his crate or dog bed, he should be left alone. If the puppy is continually handled and bothered whenever he attempts to take a nap, he may eventually become possessive over those resting areas, or be on guard when the children are home. People have told us that they can't touch their dog when he is sleeping, and when they do, he growls at them. It is most likely that this dog has been bothered quite a bit and has hit a threshold. Puppies *do* look adorable when they are sleeping, but they need to be left alone. You would never permit your children to wake your newborn up when asleep. When you put your toddler down for a nap, you tiptoe around the house and do not bother the child unless absolutely necessary. If you need to move the child, you do so gently and quietly. We would not lie on top of a resting child or poke and prod at the child simply because we can. If you have a very young puppy who is growling when you attempt to pick him up from the bed or calmly and gently pet him, you should be concerned. This is not typical behavior and should be discussed with a professional in the field.

Give the Dog a Break

Many problems occur in families with young dogs and children because the dog never gets to rest. Between the adults, the children, the children's friends, the dog is constantly being handled. Dogs need a break from people constantly touching them. When your dog is still and resting, it's because he needs to rest—tell the children to leave him alone. You need to let him take the break that he requires. Explain that he is tired. You can discuss with older children how *they* feel when they are tired—cranky and grumpy, and not up to doing much or interacting with anyone. Younger children will probably not understand, so if it makes it easier for the children and for you, put the dog in his crate for a nap.

Do not feel badly about sending him to his crate. This is not a punishment, and your dog will not think of it in that way. He will probably be glad to finally have a place where he can rest and not be bothered. It is very important that the children leave the dog alone when he is in his crate. He needs a safe haven where he can go to get away from the excitement and commotion and not be worried about being stepped on, fallen on, or picked up from a sound sleep.

Puppies, like children, tire and need naps or quiet times.

Problems in General

We cannot stress enough the importance of seeking professional help if you are experiencing *any* problems with your puppy, especially problems similar to those mentioned above. We are often amazed at how many times a person will say, "I felt uncomfortable, about that," "I didn't think he should be doing that," or "I knew something was wrong," but they did nothing about it because they weren't sure. Their gut instinct was right—always go with it. If something makes you uncomfortable, then chances are it's not a good thing. Please refer to the Appendix in the back of this book and get professional help. The risk is too high to let it go, especially with children in the house. They are the ones who will likely be on the receiving end of whatever the puppy decides to do when enough is enough. These problems don't happen with most puppies, but we want you to be aware of the potential. If you are well informed and prepared, you can prevent problems from occurring.

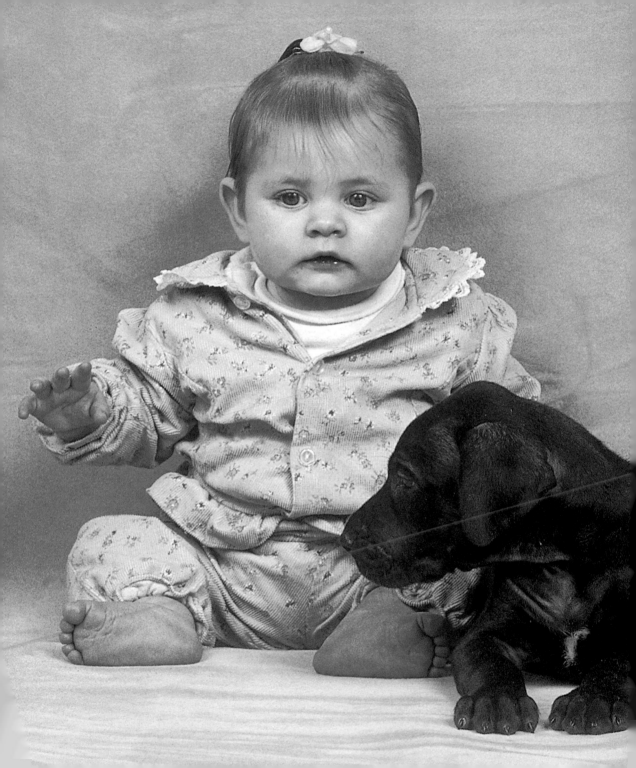

"The dog was created specially for children. He is a god of frolic."
—Henry Ward Beecher

Section 5

Preparing Your Dog for a New Baby

Chapter 13
Getting Your Puppy or Dog Ready for a Baby

Chapter 13

Getting Your Puppy or Dog Ready for a Baby

Many dog owners face a time in their lives when the size of their family will change with the addition of an infant or child. They are very often concerned about how their dog will react to this new human family member.

You *can* bring a baby into your home with your dogs, but we thought, would the majority of dog owners facing this issue know what to do? Could they make it work?

The information in this chapter is designed to help you prepare your puppy or dog for the new arrival. It is also important and useful for those who do not have children of their own, but will have frequent visits by the infants or children of other people (grandchildren, nieces/nephews, friend's children, etc.). The important thing is to start as early as possible enforcing the behavior you would like to see from your dog around children.

If you have a puppy or young dog who will need to cope with a little person living in the home, the best advice we can give is to start *now* by teaching and insisting on good manners. Follow everything that has been outlined in this book. A puppy can be easier than an adult dog in some ways because a puppy will not have been with you as long. The routines you are developing for him are still new, and he probably has not learned as many bad habits that will need to be fixed. You can start off right by teaching the puppy how you would like him to behave in all situations and around all types and ages of people.

YOU'RE IN CHARGE

Starting with a Good Foundation

Several years ago, Lynn found herself in this exact situation. She and her husband were expecting their first child, and had three adult dogs in the household (ages 10, 5, and 1 year). How would the dogs react to the new baby? Working professionally in the field of dog training and behavior, she knew the importance of socialization. Over the years, her dogs had received a great deal of socialization with the children of family members and friends, both in and outside their home. But how would they react to spending 24 hours a day, 7 days a week with a baby? The temperament of her dogs and all of the work she had done establishing house rules (no furniture access and no running) and providing constant obedience training for good manners (no jumping up) were critical. When the baby came home, the dogs showed excitement and interest, but things slowly went back to normal (well…as normal as things can be with a new baby in the home!). The baby coming home was not that difficult for her dogs because their routine did not significantly change, nor did they lose any privileges that they previously had. Their lives basically went on as usual, except for some change in the amount of time and attention they received.

If you have an adult dog who has been with you for a number of years, it can sometimes be more difficult to bring a baby or child home. This will depend on several things:

- The dog's personality and temperament
- How much socialization the dog has received throughout his life with infants, toddlers, and young children
- How your dog reacts around children who have come to visit or when he sees them on his daily walks
- How much training have you done with your dog to ensure that he has good house manners

- Whether or not your dog is on a daily routine that will have to stop once the baby arrives (e.g., jogging 2 miles every morning with mom)
- Whether or not your dog listens to you when you have guests over (greets guests calmly), or when you want him off the bed or sofa

Start now by teaching and insisting on good manners.

Remember, your adult dog has been accustomed to having you all to himself, maybe for several years. It may not be easy for him to suddenly have to share your time with a new child or infant.

House Rules for Dogs

We have mentioned a number of times throughout this book that you should establish some house rules for your dogs and enforce them. Do not wait until the baby is in your home to decide that your dog is not behaving the way you would like and suddenly decide he must change *now*. Below are some rules that, if established now, will benefit you in the long run.

When Indoors, Calmness Reigns

If you have multiple dogs living with you, don't allow dog-to-dog play in the house. One dog roughhousing or wrestling with another can have the same negative outcome as a running dog. Dog-to-dog play is an outdoor activity. We also discourage rough play and wrestling between older children and dogs, as previously discussed. We do on occasion play with our dogs in the house, but it is *controlled* play, on our terms, and ends when we say it ends.

A running dog or multiple dogs playing and roughhousing in the house can be especially dangerous if you have an infant lying on the floor or older baby just starting to crawl. At a certain stage in an infant's development, she needs to be given some floor time to learn how to push herself up, develop arm strength, and learn to roll over from belly to back and vice versa. Dogs who are running, wrestling, and chasing one another or an older child will not notice or care about the infant on the floor. The infant will end up being stepped on, knocked over, scratched by toenails, and possibly injured and frightened by the experience.

CASE STUDY
Teach Your Dog What Is Off-Limits

Pia received a frantic call for help from the owners of a 2-year-old active Rhodesian Ridgeback named Clover. Clover had constant attention from mom and dad, since both worked as architects from their home. They were diligent about training, bringing Clover to a puppy class at 12 weeks of age, and continuing on with her training for the first year of her life. Mom-to-be Dena had to be on bed rest during the last 3 months of her pregnancy, so Clover's training slacked off. Clover was getting more and more rambunctious, and spent a good deal of her day running around the house, entertaining herself. Her all-time favorite daily event was when the mail carrier arrived. She would wait on their bed upstairs, looking out the window. When the truck pulled up, she bolted down the stairs in a barking frenzy, jumping up and scratching at the front door. Anytime the doorbell rang or Clover heard someone at the front door, she bolted toward the door. They never really got control over this behavior, but didn't see it as a serious problem until one day their infant was lying on the floor in Clover's path. Clover ran right over the baby, and sent the infant flying across the hardwood floor. Fortunately the baby received no injuries, but immediate training was required! Clover was taught to walk to the front door and sit. She was also taught that the baby's blanket was off limits and, if it was on the floor, she had to walk around it (we'll show you how to teach this later in this chapter). It also helped to change her attitude once she learned that the mail carrier brought doggy biscuits. Life went on more peacefully after that.

When in the house, insist that the dog is calm and try to prevent your dog from becoming overly excited or aroused. As a general rule, if you are calm and passive, then the dog should be calm and passive. If you are sitting on the sofa reading a book or working at the computer, the dog should be resting quietly. If your dog will not lie quietly by your side, then put a crate nearby so the dog learns to be calm when you are calm. If there is a time during the day when your dog seems to be unable to control himself or remain calm, it probably means that he needs to get out for some exercise. Do yourself and your family a favor by taking a few minutes to bring the dog out to run off some of the pent-up energy by throwing a Frisbee or ball. A 10-minute game of fetch will tire out most dogs.

Furniture Access

Whether or not to allow your dog on your furniture is your own personal decision. We both have big dogs with thick long coats. Lynn does not allow her dogs on any of the furniture, because they take up a lot of space (and she doesn't want to have to clean up the hair). Pia does allow her dogs to get up on her bed, but only when she invites them. The important thing to remember with furniture access is that the dog *must* get off the furniture when told, and should only get on the furniture when invited. If you experience any problems at all when the dog is on a piece of furniture (won't get off, growls, shows teeth, etc.) please immediately contact a professional in the field. This is a serious problem, especially if you plan on bringing a child into your home.

If your dog is behaving himself and following your rules, there is no right or wrong when it comes to furniture access, but there are some things to consider.

- If you have a dog and know that someday you will have children in the home, it will be easier for your dog if you determine right from the start what the furniture rules will be for him. Will you want your dog sleeping on your child's bed, or jumping up on the sofa next to or on top of your infant who is lying there? You will spend a great deal of time sitting on the sofa to feed the baby (they eat every few hours), to

Permitting dogs on the sofa is up to you. But when asked to get off, they should respond immediately.

lay the baby down to interact with her, or simply to sit and hold the baby in your arms. If your dog has always had sofa access he will not understand why he is being yelled at when he tries to jump up on the sofa while the baby is lying on it. This is a place where he has become accustomed to sleeping, and he has never been yelled at for it in the past.

• An infant making noises and moving her arms and legs will certainly bring out the curiosity in the pup. Don't be surprised if a pup or older dog who has never had furniture access decides to jump up to see what is going on. People will tell us over and over again that their dog never gets up on furniture. However, if the dog has the free run of the house, there is no guarantee that the dog will not make himself cozy when you are not there.

• If your dog does have sofa access, and you would like that to continue, there is nothing wrong with inviting him up while you are sitting on the sofa holding the baby. Let him see that he can still have this access, provided he listens to you and gets on and off when told. You can show him that he is still a part of your life and part of the family. (*Please note that the dog should only be invited up with you and the baby provided your dog has not given you any reason to be concerned about how he might act toward the baby.*) If you decide that you no longer want the dog on the sofa, then you should teach him to remain off the sofa well before the baby arrives. Dogs *can* learn new rules. If you suddenly decide to change the rules, make sure you are rewarding the dog for lying next to the sofa, and do not become upset with him if he should periodically jump up. He will make mistakes. Any time you attempt to change a behavior, it will take time. The dog will have no understanding why the rules have changed, so patience is the key.

Any time you attempt to change a behavior, it will take time.

The easiest solution for preventing unwanted furniture access problems is to simply not allow the dog up on the furniture from the onset, and always supervise.

Kitchen Table and Counters

From the moment you get your dog you should teach him proper kitchen manners—how he should behave when the family is sitting at the table eating or when you are preparing meals. Most nuisance behaviors occur in the kitchen, since we spend a great deal of time there, and this is where food is kept and eaten. Do not allow your dog to reach up on the table or counter, beg for food, nudge your arms and hands, or paw at you while you are eating or preparing food. If they are in the kitchen or dining room with you, they should be lying down and calm. They can be wandering around as long as they are not annoying people and begging for food. It is important to recognize that you will probably, someday, have children in your home (yours or your guests). Children do not eat quite as neatly as adults. Older babies and young toddlers tend to spill and drop more food onto their chairs, highchairs, themselves, and the floor than actually makes it to their mouths. If your dog does not have good manners at the dinner table, he may end up in a feeding frenzy off your child's lap. Not pleasant for the child or good practice for your dog. (There are, of course, benefits to having a dog around when young children are eating. Dogs make great vacuum cleaners and mops.)

Your dog jumping up on the kitchen table or counters is a safety issue for the baby. You might have your child in a baby carrier up on the table or counter as you are preparing food or feeding her. If your dog is jumping up onto these surfaces, his paws can easily scratch the baby or even worse, cause the carrier to tip.

Take Care of Your Dog on *Your* Schedule

Teach your dog that his needs (eating, going for walks, exercise sessions, etc.) will be taken care of on your schedule, when *you* are ready. If your dog is accustomed to a regular schedule for his everyday activities, you should start to vary that schedule. Have you ever noticed that your dog seems to know when it's dinnertime? He looks at you in the kitchen as if to say, "Hey, it's 6:00 p.m., aren't you going to feed me now?" Do not get into the habit of catering to your dog when he tells you it's time for a walk or for him to be fed. It is not likely that you will be able to maintain the same schedule when your baby comes home. Things will have to happen when they happen. It will be easier for your dog to adjust if he is already accustomed to a varying schedule.

> **From the moment you get your dog, you should teach him proper kitchen manners.**

Baby-Specific Training and Preparation

Having a trained dog who will listen and respond to you and has been taught good manners is even more critical when you have a baby or young child in the home. Please refer back to the obedience training section in Chapter 6 on teaching the puppy his name, not to jump up, and how to take treats gently from your hand. Below are some additional training exercises that will be invaluable with a new baby in the house.

Walking Properly on Leash

If you are preparing for the arrival of an infant, you probably have, or will eventually purchase, a baby stroller. Walking is one of the best forms of exercise to help get moms back in shape after giving birth, and the stroller ride is fun for the baby as well. Take your newborn and your dog for a walk together, and you can all reap the benefits—fresh air and exercise at the same time. A lovely picture, right? It can happen for you, but you need to start *now*.

You cannot allow your dog to drag you on leash every time you go for walks together, and then expect him to not pull just because you are pushing a baby stroller. Please take your dog to an obedience training class or hire a private trainer to help you teach your dog proper leash manners. Once you have done that, practice every day, and take the dog for walks with the baby stroller, even if the baby has not yet arrived. Sure, your neighbors might wonder what you are doing, but it is safer to practice with your dog and the empty stroller, in case your dog pulls you to chase a squirrel while your hands are on the stroller handle. If the dog pulls very suddenly and catches you off guard, he could cause the stroller to tip over. Once the baby arrives, your dog will enjoy and look forward to going for walks with you and the

A pleasant family walk can be good for everyone.

baby. The dog's routine stays the same, and he still gets to spend time having fun with you and now the baby as well. Your dog will love seeing the stroller come out—it means everyone is going for a walk.

Walk Around the Blanket

You will spend a lot of time playing on the floor with an infant in your home. For most dog owners, as soon they sit on the floor, the dog thinks it's an invitation to come over for petting and play and to get in their laps. Try to get your dog accustomed to you being on the floor, but not interacting with him. Get a baby doll. Spread a baby blanket out on the floor and put the doll on the blanket. Talk to the doll and interact with it like you might do with an infant while your dog is in the room. Do not allow your dog to put a paw on the baby blanket or, especially, walk across it. He may come over to see what you are doing, but must remain calm. Teach him to lie down on the floor *next to the blanket*, and to *walk around the blanket* to

225

Teach your dog to be calm while you interact with your baby on the floor.

get to the other side. The blanket is off limits to the dog. Babies need a lot of floor time, and you will feel more relaxed knowing that, if your baby is on the floor, your dog will not walk over her.

Remember the story about Clover? Clover was taught to walk around the blanket and "Get back" when too close. Here is how you can train your dog to do the same.

Teach "Around"

You can easily do this by putting a small blanket on the floor. Start with your puppy or dog close to you. With a treat in one hand in front of your dog's nose, lure the dog around the blanket. If the dog steps on the blanket make sure you are not luring the dog too close to the blanket. Once he is half way around the blanket, tell him, "Yes!" and give him the treat. Show him another treat, and lure him the rest of the way. As your dog becomes more proficient, lure him around the entire blanket and give the treat at the end once he is back next to you. You can now add a verbal cue, such as "Around." Once your dog is walking around the blanket in one direction, teach him to walk around it in the other direction. All dogs, like people, have a weaker side, so it may be easier for him to go in one direction than the other. Do not give the treat if his paws touch the blanket. When your dog is easily walking around the blanket, remove the treat from your hand and use the same hand cue. You can reward him from your pocket instead.

Teach "Get Back"

Start with your dog facing you in a standing position. Hold a treat in your hand at your dog's nose level, making sure his nose is not up in the air or he will sit. Take one step toward your dog, moving the treat toward his face, as you say, "Get back." Your dog will probably take one step backward since you are walking into his space. As soon as he moves backwards, even slightly, tell him, "Yes!" and give him the treat. Gradually add more steps. Once he understands the behavior, stand still. Using the same hand signal say, "Get back." If your dog moves back, tell him, "Yes!" and toss him the treat. Eventually you will need to do this when you are sitting in a chair and then on the floor, since you may be on the blanket with the baby. If your dog does not back up, walk into him to reinforce what you said.

The sound of a crying baby can bring about many different reactions from a dog.

Crying Baby

The sound of a crying baby can bring about many different reactions from a dog. Some dogs become very excited, some concerned, and others more nervous. Lynn had three adult dogs when her first child arrived, two males and a female. In the beginning, when the baby would cry, her female dog would immediately get up and go to the room where the baby was and, if Lynn wasn't there, she would come to find her. She would look as if to say, "Hey, the baby needs you, can't you hear it? Get in there!" Her two male dogs had very little reaction to the crying—it did not seem to bother them in any way. For some dogs, crying doesn't seem to bother them until you make your move toward the baby—then you have ignited their interest. Eventually, dogs learn that the sound of the baby means someone will go to the infant. You can help to get your dog used to the sound of a baby crying by playing a tape or CD of that sound. Put the tape player in the room where the baby will spend most of her time, and periodically play the tape. When the crying occurs, react calmly and go to the room where the sound is coming from. You can even keep a baby doll in that room to pick up and hold when you get there. Show your dog there is no reason to become alarmed or excited and that everything is fine. If your dog learns that when the baby cries, everyone runs to the baby, then he will simply do what everyone else is doing.

Preparing Your Dog for the Actions of Children

As you recall from Chapter 10, dogs do not view children or infants the

At any age, children love to hug puppies.

same as they do adults. Children have very different body language from that of adults, and are much more unpredictable in their movements. You should never assume that, just because your dog is fine with adults, he will be fine around children or a crawling baby. Please also refer back to Chapter 4 on socialization to be sure your puppy or dog is getting sufficient and proper socialization with children to help him prepare for the arrival of your baby.

Physical contact with a dog by young children is different from that of adults. Young children do not have as much control over their arms and might whack the dog instead of pet him. Never assume that your infant cannot hurt your dog. Babies have an amazingly strong grip. When they get hold of something with their hands, they grasp on and do not let go. Many a dog has lost a chunk of hair from the grip of an infant!

Children hug a lot. Some children will hug their dogs ten times per day or more. Try to get your dog accustomed to being hugged by you, and take note of his reaction. If he cannot handle or dislikes this behavior from you, he definitely will not want it from a child.

Your Dog's Toys: Finding a Place

As discussed earlier, problems can arise from having too many toys spread out all over the floor. We also explained the benefits of keeping your dog's toys in a toy box. Do not wait until your baby comes home from the hospital to decide that you are not going to allow your dog's things to be all over the floor. Start now by creating a dog toy box and keeping all of his things there.

From the moment the baby comes home there will be lots of new toys for the baby. Many of them may be made of a similar material to toys that you have given your dog. How will he know that he is not supposed to take the baby's stuffed teddy bear that is on the floor where his toys are usually found? Help to set him up for success and make the transition as smooth as possible.

Baby Talk

Many dog owners, especially those who do not have children, tend to use baby talk with their puppies, and it usually continues even as the dog becomes older. The dog becomes accustomed to the soft, cooing, sweet voice that has always been directed at him. The same families now bring a baby home and start talking to the baby in the same manner. It is not a surprise that the dog immediately comes running at the sound of the baby talk, since it was normally meant for him. The owners become frustrated that every time they try to cuddle and coo with their baby, the dog gets in the way or wants to be in the middle. The dog also becomes frustrated because he does not understand why he is being shoved aside for responding to the voice that normally meant attention for him. If you know there will some day be a baby in the family, you can help avoid confusion by starting off talking to your puppy in a normal voice, rather than using baby talk. If this is difficult for you, as we know it is for many, then don't become upset with your dog. Remain calm, give him a nice rub behind the ear. Remember that you control when and how much petting and attention a dog receives, so don't feel guilty.

Bring Baby Things Home from Hospital

To help prepare your dog for the arrival of your baby, it can be helpful to get the dog used to the baby's scent. When the baby is born, have someone bring a blanket or t-shirt home that was used on the baby. Let the dog smell the baby item and carry it around with you, placing it in the bassinet, changing table, and crib. You can even sit on the sofa and hold it in your lap while you watch television or read a book. By the time the baby comes home, the dog will have become familiar with her scent.

Baby Seat in the Car

In Chapter 3, we discussed ways to safely transport your dog in your car (crate, dog seatbelt harness). If your dog has been riding loose in the back seat of the car, able to move from side to side, front seat to back, you should change this as soon as possible. You will now have an infant in a car seat on the back seat of the car. If your dog and baby are in the car together, you will not be able to prevent your dog from bothering with or jumping on the baby in her car seat. This can be a very dangerous situation. If you become worried or distracted, you will not be able to safely drive, and the risk for an accident is much higher. Consider implementing a safer means of transporting your dog in the car now, before the baby gets home.

It can be helpful to get the dog used to the baby's scent.

Baby Comes Home

Your baby is finally coming home from the hospital. It is a very exciting and hectic time for the whole family. If this is your first baby, you are likely to be a bit nervous and stressed at the thought of bringing the baby home and learning how to care for her.

Seeing Mom

Your dog will be very excited to see mom, who has probably been gone for a few days in the hospital; but chances are that mom will be preoccupied with the new baby. We typically recommend that another adult carry the baby inside so mom has a chance to greet the dog. Once the dog is calm, then the baby can go back into mom's arms. If your dog is young and has been alone for several hours on arrival day, you may want someone to take the dog out in the backyard for a romp or a good hearty walk to get rid of any pent-up energy before you introduce the dog to the baby. Do the best you can to give your dog some attention during this hectic time, and try to alternate responsibility for baby and dog care between the adult family members. Try as much as possible to prevent becoming panicked and worried about what might happen to the baby, and don't yell at the dog before he has even done anything wrong.

Let Your Dog Sniff

Babies are fragile innocent beings, and the utmost care and common sense must be used at all times when dogs and babies are interacting. Many people become overly cautious and protective of the baby, and will not let the dog near the infant. This only causes the dog to become more frustrated and even more excited and determined to meet the little one. There is nothing wrong with letting your dog sniff your baby. (*Of course common sense must be used here. If you have concerns about your dog's behavior in that he has behaved aggressively toward children or babies in the past, please consult a professional in the field for help as soon as you find out that you are pregnant. Do not wait until a month before the baby comes home.*) Your dog is curious and would like to see what this new creature is about. Tell your dog to sit and bend down to the height of your dog's head while holding the baby in your arms to let him look and sniff. Do not hold the baby too high or the dog might want to jump up to get a better look. You can also sit on the sofa and let the dog walk up and sniff the baby in your lap. If the dog is well behaved and is allowed furniture access, invite the dog onto the sofa next to you and insist he lie down. Most dogs will be very excited about the first baby coming home, and will want to sniff. Encourage the dog to sniff the baby and once done, and the excitement wears off, the dog will go back to his business. If you do not let him check out the baby, it may frustrate him.

Do the best you can to give your dog some attention during this hectic time.

Include the Dog in Activities with the Baby

Try to include your dog in as many activities with your baby or child as possible. We already mentioned in this chapter that a great family activity is to take your dog and baby for stroller walks together. You will also spend a lot of time on the floor with your infant, and you can teach your dog that he can be with you provided he remains calm and follow the rules discussed above.

231

CASE STUDY

The Dog Who Wanted To Be in the Middle of Everything

Pia's neighbor called to talk about their 12-month-old daughter and their one-and-a-half-year-old dog Champ. Both adults worked full time, spending over 3 hours a day commuting to and from work. The precious time they had at night was certainly not enough for a baby, Champ, and themselves. Their major frustration was that Champ always had to be in the middle of every interaction they had with the baby, and he was constantly stealing the baby's toys and food. If they put Champ in another room, he howled and carried on. They felt like they were always saying, "No" to the dog, but nothing seemed to be working. Champ was quite playful and enjoyed playing with them as well as the child. When the child was put to sleep at night, the two adults sat on the floor with Champ and played games with him. Champ's toys were quite similar to the child's toys, the area where they played with Champ was the same area where they played with the child, and their tone of voice when playing with the dog and child, were exactly the same. How was Champ supposed to know when it was *his* time for attention? Hearing the soft baby tones that they spoke to the child only encouraged Champ to come over, since he wasn't aware it was directed at the child and not him. How was he to know which toys were his and which ones belonged to the baby when they were all on the floor together?

After explaining it to them from the dog's point of view, they had a better understanding of how Champ was feeling and why he was behaving the way he was. He wasn't jealous of the baby, he simply wanted to be part of the fun. The dog was taught to lie down and stay, so he could still be part of the interaction, but not in the middle. Then Champ was invited to join in and taught to leave objects when told. After learning a few commands, Champ was more relaxed, the parents began enjoying him once more, and the pressure was off all of them.

Baby Playpen/Activity Center

When it comes to your baby or child, you should always think safety—especially with an infant and dog in the house. You will need a safe place to put your baby when it is time for you to leave the room (answer the phone, use the bathroom, take a shower, etc.). The safest place for the baby is probably in her crib; but because newborns cannot crawl or roll over yet, many people will leave them on a blanket on the sofa or on the

Do not allow the dog to push his way in— he may join only when invited.

floor while they step out of the room for a moment. This would be safe if you did not have dogs in the house. This may seem like simple common sense to us all, but it's worth mentioning. Never assume that your dog will go around your baby when she is lying on the floor; or that he won't put his feet up on the sofa to check her out. We have known many dogs to actually walk over a baby on the floor, sometimes stepping on them (remember Clover!), sometimes not. Babies, as they grow, need more floor time to learn how to crawl, roll over, and lift themselves up. Consider purchasing a baby playpen to use for your baby during times when you will not be right next to her. Perhaps you are preparing dinner and want to have the baby on a blanket on the floor in the kitchen. Even though the baby is in the same room with you, if you are not on the floor with her, she could be at risk of being stepped on by the dog. Putting the baby in a playpen will keep the dog from reaching her and give the baby a safe area to explore.

Swing

Many people use indoor motorized baby swings to keep their infant entertained and occupied during busy times. From a puppy or dog's

Setting your dog up for success will make the baby's arrival go much more smoothly.

perspective, this swinging, moving object looks quite interesting and can certainly motivate them to try to stop or grab hold of it. Obviously, this is not something that you would want when the baby is in it. Therefore, if you decide to use a swing, make sure you get your dog acclimated to its movement with a doll in it at first. The dog must learn to stay out of the way and not attempt to go near it when it is moving.

There is a fair amount of change that will happen in your lives and your dog's life when a new baby or child comes into the picture. Try to alleviate as much stress as possible for your dog by following the rules and guidelines discussed above, and setting your dog up for success many months *before* the arrival of the child. It will make the transition go much more smoothly and easily for everyone.

Afterword

Dogs and kids are as American as Grandma's apple pie. But what may have seemed effortless for Grandma was really the result of years of experience and testing. Knowing her apples, the proper ingredients, and how to mix them was key to making the perfect pie, and Grandma knew it!

Much like there is a recipe for "perfect" apple pie, there is a formula for developing a healthy relationship between children and their dogs—it doesn't just happen when you put them together. There are real issues that must be considered for the safety and well-being of your family. Children can get physically hurt and pets can get blamed for things that could have been easily avoided. You must follow the rules and practice the "canine" lessons given in this book if you want to avoid the chaos that will surely ensue if you don't. Too often, the initially beloved pet ends up in the shelter and the heartbroken children never understand what went wrong.

The do's and don'ts of dogs and children living together are given to us by two people who know the importance of having a well-behaved dog in the household—and all the gifts that come with it. Teaching kids to learn "dog" will not only help them become more caring, responsible humans, but will give them an opportunity to explore the world from a four-legged perspective.

Pia and Lynn have the credentials and experience to help families find harmony with their pet. Now they've shared with you their extensive knowledge of canine behavior and personal experiences raising new puppies. All you have to do is follow the "recipe" and reap the rewards of providing a loving environment where both children and dogs are cherished family members.

—Elizabeth McCorkle, President, St. Hubert's Animal Welfare Center

"Dogs are not our whole life, but they make our lives whole."
—Roger Caras

About the Authors

Pia Silvani

Pia's first involvement with dogs was rescuing a 6-year-old Golden Retriever that was going to be put to sleep because he had bitten the family children several times. The dog was very nontrusting of children, so she worked on rebuilding his trust, and provided him with guidance and leadership. He never had another incident. He learned to enjoy the company of her two nephews, and they became best of friends; he had a renewed faith in "little people." Pia's love of teaching began over 20 years ago as a private trainer, dance instructor, track and field and swimming coach for the Special Olympics, and Regional Clinician for an international aerobics corporation where she trained new instructors. After 13 years of paralegal/office management work, she decided to make her part-time teaching career a full-time dream. She combined her love of teaching people with her fondness of dogs. Pia is currently the Director of Training and Behavior at St. Hubert's Animal Welfare Center in Madison, New Jersey. She conducts private consultations specializing in aggressive and anxiety-related problems. Pia shares her home with best friend and husband, Marty, as well as their 6-year-old Belgian Tervuren, Lance, and Lance's daughter, Guinevere.

Lynn Eckhardt

Lynn's first dog, aside from the family dogs she grew up with, was a small mixed breed who she adopted from an animal shelter over 24 years ago. Since then, she has owned seven more dogs of various breeds, all raised from young pups. She began training her dogs as a hobby for various types of competitions: herding, agility, and obedience to name a few. Her love of dogs and interest in dog training and animal behavior, coupled with the desire to help others train their dogs, turned her hobby into a career. She now works teaching obedience training classes and conducting private consultations primarily on dog aggression issues. Lynn lives with her husband Tim and their two toddlers Matthew and Sydney; their cat Muggsy, and three dogs, Strider (10 months), Kobe (6 years), and Jordan (10 years).

Appendix A

Professionals in the Field

Throughout this book, we have recommended that you seek the advice of a professional in the field. This Appendix will help educate you on deciding what type of professional will best suit your needs. The following is a general description of what each professional typically does. We recommend that you ask to see a resume or inquire into the amount of education the person has acquired over the years in ethology and learning theory. Ask for references from past clients or other sources, if available. Understanding the methodology and philosophy of the person is of the utmost importance. We also like to see that the person is actively involved with professional organizations such as the Animal Behavior Society (ABS), the American College of Veterinary Behaviorists (ACVB), the American Veterinary Society of Animal Behavior (AVSAB), National Association of Dog Obedience Instructors (NADOI), Association of Pet Dog Trainers (APDT), Certified Pet Dog Training (CCPDT), and more.

Applied Animal Behaviorist

A person who instructs dog owners with a goal to change, suppress, or alter behaviors. These behaviors can range from nuisance behaviors to aggressive behaviors. This person will have a graduate level education (Masters or Ph.D.) in the field of animal behavior. The Animal Behavior Society (ABS) is a professional organization for the study of animal behavior and certifies applied animal behaviorists at the Associate level (Masters degree) or Full (Ph.D. or veterinarian with at least 5 years of clinical experience). Certified Applied Animal Behaviorists possess graduate-level education in ethology, learning theory, comparative psychology, psychology, biology, zoology, animal science, and experimental design, and a minimum of 3 to 5 years of experience. This person may specialize in a variety of pet species, including dogs, cats, birds, ferrets, horses, rabbits, and rodents.

Behavior Counselor/Behavior Consultant

A person who instructs dog owners with a goal to change, suppress, or alter behaviors. These behaviors can range from nuisance behaviors to aggressive behaviors. Anyone can call himself or herself a behaviorist. There is only one organization that certifies *applied animal behaviorists* (the ABS) and one that certifies *veterinary behaviorists* (the ACVB). This is not to say that the behavior counselor may not be qualified. There are many dog trainers and certified dog trainers who are highly qualified to work on difficult behavior problems. Once again, we suggest that you ask for referrals. Anyone working in the field of behavior must be familiar with canine social behavior and how dogs learn.

Certified Pet Dog Trainer (CPDT)

A dog trainer who trains dogs or instructs dog owners typically for pay or as a career. In order to sit for the exam, the trainer must have at least 300 hours of dog training experience within the last 5 years (225 hours or 75 percent of that time must be actual teaching time in a class or private setting as a Head Trainer, and 75 hours or 25 percent can be in other areas, such as shelter work, assisting in classes, working as a vet technician and groomer). The Certification Council for Pet Dog Trainers is a certification organization that conducts a certification program to evaluate the competency of those taking the test. Certification is similar to credentialing. The content of the exam covers instructor skills, animal husbandry, ethology, learning theory, and equipment. Prior to taking the exam, the dog trainer must have three letters of referrals from a veterinarian, client, and colleague who are willing to certify that the candidate is a professional and exhibits the knowledge necessary to sit for the test. Those passing the exam must be recertified every 3 years and maintain at least 36 continuing educational credits, proving that their focus is to provide high-valued and professional services to the general public as a result of their advanced knowledge. Please visit the web sites of the Council at www.ccpdt.com or the Association of Pet Dog Trainers, an organization that endorses the concept of certification, at www.apdt.com. (Note: While there are many schools and organizations that certify dog trainers, they are only being certified under that particular school or organization and not on a national level. Please question whether the person is certified on a national level or by the school they attended, since there are schools that teach harsh, old-fashioned methods and not methodologies based on the humane treatment of animals, as outlined in the Professional Standards for Dog Trainers.)

Dog Trainer

A person who either works directly with dogs or people with the intent of teaching new behaviors or changing existing behaviors. The level of education varies from trainer to trainer. The years of experience that a dog trainer has does not necessarily mean that the trainer will be using the most up-to-date, humane training methods or be able to change problem behaviors. The field of dog training is rapidly growing. Before seeking the assistance of a dog trainer, we recommend that you inquire about their methodologies and obtain references. Please refer to Delta Society's *Professional Standards for Dog Trainers: Effective, Humane Principles.* This published book can be obtained online at www.deltasociety.org or, for more information, contact them at Delta Society, 289 Perimeter Road East, Renton, WA 98055-1329 (e-mail: info@deltasociety.org). (Note: Anyone can call himself or herself a dog trainer. Therefore, we recommend, for the safety and well-being of your dog, that you are diligent in your research about trainers before hiring them.)

Veterinarian

A person with education in the field of veterinary medicine. Their specialty is in the field of medical and/or surgical procedures on animals. Many veterinarians specialize, like medical doctors, in various fields or with specific animals. Typically, you would look for a small-animal practitioner, but many veterinarians work with both large (e.g., horses, cows) and small (dogs, cats) animals.

Veterinary Behaviorist

A person who instructs dog owners with a goal to change, suppress, or alter behaviors. These behaviors can range from nuisance behaviors to aggressive behaviors. A veterinary behaviorist is a veterinarian with advanced education in the field of animal behavior (a minimum of 2-year residency under the guidance of a board-certified veterinarian), and is professionally certified by the American College of Veterinary Behaviorists. The Veterinary Behaviorist is knowledgeable in psychopharmacology and may incorporate drug therapy into a behavioral treatment regimen.

Appendix B

Resources

Organizations

American College of Veterinary Behaviorists (ACVB)
Texas A&M University
College Station TX 77843-4474
E-mail: info@DACVB.ORG

American Humane Association (AHA)
63 Inverness Drive East
Englewood, CO 80112
Telephone: (303) 792-9900
www.americanhumane.org

American Kennel Club (AKC)
5580 Centerview Drive
Raleigh, NC 27606
Telephone: (919) 233-9767
E-mail: info@akc.org
www.akc.org

American Society for the Prevention of Cruelty to Animals (ASPCA)
424 E. 92nd Street
New York, NY 10128-6804
Telephone: (212) 876-7700
www.aspca.org

Animal Behavior Society (ABS)

Indiana University
2611 East 10th Street #170
Bloomington, IN 47408-2603
Telephone: (812) 856-5541
E-mail:aboffice@indiana.edu
www.animalbehavior.org

Association of Pet Dog Trainers

150 Executive Center Drive, Box 35
Greenville, SC 29615
Telephone: (800) PET-DOGS
E-mail: information@apdt.com
www.apdt.com

Canadian Kennel Club (CKC)

89 Skyway Avenue, Suite 100
Etobicoke, Ontario
M9W 6R4 Canada
Telephone: (416) 675-5511
E-mail: information@ckc.ca
www.cvc.ca

Canadian Association of Professional Pet Dog Trainers (CAPPDT)

P.O. Box 59011,
Whitby, Ontario
Canada, L1N 0A4
Telephone: (877) SIT-STAY
E-mail: webmaster@cappdt.ca
www.cappdt.ca

Certification Council for Pet Dog Trainers (CCPDT)

Professional Testing Corporation
1350 Broadway, 17th Floor
New York, NY 10018
Telephone: (212) 356-0682
E-mail: joan@ccpdt.org

Delta Society
580 Naches Avenue, SW,
Suite 101
Renton, WA 98055-2297
Telephone: (425) 226-7357
E-mail: info@deltasociety.org
www.deltasociety.org

**The Humane Society of the
United States (HSUS)**
2100 L Street NW
Washington, DC 20037
Telephone: (202) 452-1100
www.hsus.org

The Kennel Club
1 Charges Street
London, England
W1J 8AB
Telephone: 0870 606 6750
www.the-kennel-club.org.uk

**Royal Society for the Prevention
of Cruelty to Animals (RSPCA)**
Telephone: 0870 3335 999
www.rspca.org.uk

United Kennel Club (UKC)
100 E. Kilgore Road
Kalamazoo, MI 49002-5584
Telephone:(269) 34309020
E-mail: pbickell@ukcdogs.com
www.ukcdogs.com

Useful Web Sites

American College of Veterinary Behaviorists (ACVB)
www.dacvb.org
The ACVB is a 501(c)3 organization recognized by the American Board of Veterinary Specialists (ABVS) of the American Veterinary Medical Association (AVMA) as the official certifying organization for veterinary behavioral specialists. The ABVS recognizes 23 different veterinary specialties, from internal medicine to pathology, from ophthalmology to microbiology. The primary objectives of the ACVB are to advance veterinary behavioral science, increase the competency of those who practice in this field, and protect and serve the public.

American Society for Prevention of Cruelty to Animals (ASPCA)
www.aspca.org
A privately funded 501©(3) not-for-profit corporation that provides effective means for the prevention of cruelty to animals throughout the United States. The ASPCA offers national programs in humane education, public awareness, government advocacy, shelter support, and animal medical services and placement.

Animal Behavior Associates
www.AnimalBehaviorAssociates.com
Certified, degreed applied animal behaviorists helping to build relationships with your pets one step at a time. Services offered for the pet professional as well as the pet owners. Developers of the Pet Wellness Program, assisting you in having a behaviorally healthy pet through online telecourses as well as written materials.

The Animal Behavior Society (ABS)
www.animalbehavior.org
The Animal Behavior Society is a nonprofit scientific society, founded to encourage and promote the study of animal behavior. ABS members are from

all over the world, but primarily from North, Central, and South America. Founded in 1964, the organization promotes the study of animal behavior in the broadest sense, including studies using descriptive and experimental methods under natural and controlled conditions.

Association of Pet Dog Trainers (APDT)
www.apdt.com

A professional organization of individual trainers committed to becoming better trainers through education. The APDT offers individual pet dog trainers a respected and concerted voice in the dog world. The organization continues to promote professional trainers to the veterinary profession and to increase public awareness of dog-friendly training techniques.

Certification Council for Pet Dog Trainers (CCPDT)
www.ccpdt.com

The CCPDT is an international testing and certification program for professional pet dog trainers. The CCPDT's certification program is based on humane training practices and the latest scientific knowledge related to dog training. Competence and continued growth in training practices is promoted through the recertification of qualified professionals.

Delta Society
www.deltasociety.org

A nonprofit organization with the goal of improving human health through service and therapy animals. The Delta Society is an international organization that unites people who have mental and physical disabilities and patients in healthcare facilities with professionally trained animals to help improve their health.

Pet Finder
www.petfinder.com

A national web site to assist you in locating shelters and rescue groups currently caring for adoptable pets. Pet Finder offers a resource library and opportunities to post classified ads for lost or found pets, pets wanted, and pets needing homes.

Purdue University, Veterinary Education
www.vet.purdue.edu/animalbehavior

Their mission is to facilitate successful integration of pets in society and to strengthen the human-animal bond; to reduce the number of animals rendered to shelters or euthanized for behavior problems; and to promote humane and efficient techniques of training and behavior modification.

San Francisco SPCA
www.sfspca.org

The San Francisco SPCA is a private, nonprofit animal welfare organization dedicated to saving San Francisco's homeless cats and dogs; to helping pets stay in loving homes; and to cultivating respect and awareness for animals' rights and needs. Offers dog training classes, dog trainer academy, humane education, hearing dog program, feral cat program, and much more.

St. Hubert's Animal Welfare Center, Madison, N.J.
www.sthuberts.org

Founded in 1939 by Geraldine R. Dodge, St. Hubert's serves animals and people with a wide variety of programs that nurture the human-animal bond and foster an environment in which people respect all living creatures. The organization developed many innovative programs for animals and people, serving as models for other organizations across the country. One of the largest dog training schools in the country, pet adoptions, humane education, pet loss support groups, and much more.

References

Abrantes, Roger. *Dog Language: An Encyclopedia of Canine Behaviour.* Naperville, IL: Wakan Tanka Publishers, 1997.

Bergen, D. *Play as a Medium for Learning and Development.* Portsmouth, NH: Heinemann, 1988.

Bornstein, M., Haynes, O., Pascual, L., Painter, K., Galperin, C. "Play in two societies: pervasiveness of process, specificity of structure." *Child Development*, 70, 317-331. (1999).

Hetts, Suzanne. *Pet Behavior Protocols, What to Say, What to Do, When to Refer.* Lakewood, CO: AAHA Press, 1999.

Lindsay, Steven R. *Handbook of Applied Dog Behavior and Training, Vol. 1 and 2.* Ames, IA: Iowa State University Press, 2000.

Fein, G. "Pretend Play in Childhood: An Integrative Review." *Child Development*, pp. 1095-1118. (1981).

Fernie, David. *The Nature of Children's Play.* www.kidsource.com.

Fox, Michael. *Integrative Development of Brain and Behavior in the Dog.* Chicago, IL: University of Chicago Press, 1971.

London, Karen. "Frolicking Fidos Workshop." 2003.

McArdle, Paul. "Child: Care, Health and Development." *Children's Play*, Vol. 27:6, p 509, November 2001.

Overall, Karen. *Clinical Behavioral Medicine for Small Animals.* St. Louis, MO: Mosby, Inc., 1997.

Pfaffenberger, Clarence. *The New Knowledge of Dog Behavior.* Dogwise Publishing, reprinted 2002.

Piaget, J. *Play, Dreams, and Imitations in Childhood.* New York: Norton, 1962.

"Puppy Vaccination and Socialization Should Go Together," Anderson, Robert K., DVM. Diplomat, American College of Veterinary Preventive Medicine and Diplomat of American College of Veterinary Behaviorists, University of Minnesota, School of Public Health, Minneapolis, MN.

Purdue University, Animal Behavior Clinic statement dated December 4, 2002 by Andrew Luescher, DVM, PhD., Diplomat ACVB, Director of Animal Behavior Clinic, Purdue University and Steve Thompson, DVM, Diplomat ABVP, Certified in Canine/Feline Practice, Director of The Pet Wellness Clinic, Purdue University.

Scott, J.P. and Fuller, J.L. *Dog Behavior: The Genetic Basis*. Chicago, IL: The University of Chicago Press, 1965.

Serpell, James, *The Domestic Dog*. Cambridge, England: Cambridge University Press, 1995.

Recommended Reading

Anderson, Teoti. *The Super Simple Guide to Housetraining*. Neptune City, NJ: T.F.H. Publications, Inc., 2004.

Bailey, G. *Perfect Puppy: How to Raise a Well-Behaved Dog*. Pleasantville, NY: Reader's Digest Association, 1996.

Bohenkamp, G. *Help! My Dog Has an Attitude*. Belmont, CA: Perfect Paws, Inc., 1994.

Broitman, V. and Lipman, S., *Take a Bow Wow I and II*. Videos on trick training, 1995.

Donaldson, J. *Mine!* San Francisco, CA: Kinship Communications, 2002.

Dunbar, Ian. *Before and After Your Puppy*. Berkeley, CA: James & Kenneth Publishers, 2004.

Fogel, B. *The Encyclopedia of the Dog*. New York: Dorling Kindersley, 1993.

Hartmann-Kent, S. *Your Dog and Your Baby*. Eliot, ME: Howln Moon Press, 1999.

Hetts, S. *Introducing Your Dog to Your New Baby*. Slide presentation.

Hetts, S. and Estep, D.Q. *Raising a Behaviorally Healthy Puppy*. Littleton, CO: Island Dog Press, 2004.

Hunter, R., *Fun and Games with Dogs*. Eliot, ME: Howln Moon Press, 1993.

Kilcommons, B. and Wilson, S. *Child-Proofing Your Dog*. New York: Warner, 1994.
King, Trish. *Parenting Your Dog*. Neptune City, NJ: T.F.H. Publications, Inc., 2004.

London, K. and McConnell, P. *Way to Go!*. Black Earth, WI: Dog's Best Friend, Ltd., 2003.

McConnell, P. *How to be the Leader of the Pack*. Black Earth, WI: Dog's Best Friend, Ltd., 2002.

Nelson, L. and Pivar, G. *Management Magic*. Self, 1994.

Rutherford, C. and Neil, D.H. *How to Raise a Puppy You Can Live With*. Loveland, CO: Alpine Publishers, 1999.

Ryan, T. *Games People Play to Train their Dogs*. Kula, HI: Legacy by Mail Press, 1996.

Scidmore, B. and McConnell, P. *Puppy Primer*. Black Earth, WI: Dog's Best Friend, Ltd., 1996.

Sternberg, S., *A Guide to Choosing Your Next Dog from a Shelter*. Accord, NY: Rondout Valley Kennels, 1998. (www.suesternberg.com)

Sternberg, S. *Tricks for Treats*. Accord, NY: Rondout Valley Kennels, 1998. (www.suesternberg.com)

Walkowicz, C. *The Perfect Match: A Dog Buyer's Guide*. New York: Macmillan, 1996.

Wright, J.C. and Lashnits, J.W. *Ain't Misbehavin'*. Emmaus, PA: Rodale Press, 2001.

Other Reading

Professional Standards for Dog Trainers: Effective, Humane Principles, Sponsored by Delta Society, Printed and Funded by Pedigree, 2001.

Clothier, S. *Bones Would Rain from the Sky*. New York: Warner, 2002.

Donaldson, J. *Culture Clash*. Berkeley, CA: James & Kenneth Publishers, 1996.

McConnell, P. *The Other End of the Leash*. New York: Ballantine, 2002.

Reid, P. *Excel-erated Learning*. Berkeley, CA: James & Kenneth Publishers, 1996.

Index

Photo Credits

Lynn Becker: 183

Mary Bloom: 104

Jean Donaldson: 150

Lynn Eckhardt: 15, 27, 36, 43, 45, 54, 71, 48, 90, 99, 100, 109, 112, 118, 125, 127, 134, 136, 147, 157, 163, 166, 176, 198, 201, 203, 207, 208, 222, 225, 226, 233

Tim Eckhardt: 236

Isabelle Francais: 8, 13, 18, 20, 33, 35, 38, 42, 49, 59, 62, 64, 66, 68, 73, 77, 83, 85, 94, 96, 103, 108, 116, 123, 128, 130, 132, 140, 142, 164, 165, 168, 170, 171, 174, 181, 182, 186, 189, 214, 216, 228,234

Pia Silvani: 10, 16, 24, 51, 56, 74, 99, 134, 147, 155, 159, 169, 176, 193, 201

Candida Tomassini: 172, 196